A Beginner's Guide to Buddhism

Your Path to a Meaningful Life

&

A Beginner's Guide to Meditation

Your Path to Wisdom

Duangta Wanthong Mondi

Published by Russ Crowley

A Beginner's Guide to Buddhism & A Beginner's Guide to Meditation

http://www.teachermondi.com

Copyright © 2015 Russ Crowley, Bangkok

Edited by Russ Crowley, Red Dragon Publishing

ISBN: 978-1-908203-19-9

ISBN: 978-1515398769 (CreateSpace-assigned ISBN)

Why You Should Read This Book

I compiled these short beginner's guides to Buddhism and to meditation because they can give you both a quick overview of these subjects and help you to improve your life in a number of ways.

The first book is '*A Beginner's Guide to Buddhism: Your Path to a Meaningful Life*' and this helps to explain, in an easy to follow and understand manner, about life, about living happy, and the essentials to forge your path to a meaningful life.

Many think of Buddhism as a religion, but I think His Holiness, The XIV Dalai Lama best summed it up when he said:

> *"Don't use Buddhism to become a Buddhist.*
> *Use Buddhism to become better at whatever*
> *else in your life you are doing already."*

And that sums this book up, it will help you to become better at what you already are doing.

The second book, '*A Beginner's Guide to Meditation: Your Path to Wisdom*', will also help you in many ways. Who among us doesn't wish to be able to calm their mind, to understand and appreciate more of what's going on in our lives, how to increase our consciousness, release stress, and deal with life's pressures in a much easier manner?

Meditation is scientifically proven to help in many ways, and regular meditation will help you to take control of your life, help you to achieve everything you wish, and improve you and your life immeasurably.

About The Author

Duangta Wanthong Mondi is Thai and a Buddhist. She grew up and lives in a rural area in North-east of Thailand, where she works as an English teacher in a Thai State school. Duangta's family are also Buddhists, and her father has been an ordained Buddhist monk for over 10 years.

For more about the author and her books, refer to page II-49.

Dedicated to you.

Master Table of Contents

I. A BEGINNER'S GUIDE TO BUDDHISM

II. A BEGINNER'S GUIDE TO MEDITATION

I

A Beginner's Guide to Buddhism

Table of Contents

*The amount of happiness that you have
depends on the amount of freedom you have in
your heart.*

Thich Nhat Hanh

BUDDHA

Chapter 1.   History and Essence of Buddhism

Learning about how Buddhism began is a key step in learning and understanding more about it and its principles. Indeed, much has been written about Buddhism, but in this first chapter I give an overview of its beginnings and its key elements. This includes the history of Lord Buddha; The Threefold Training which form the backbone of the discipline, doctrine, and moral code that Lord Buddha spoke about; and, also how the principles and approach of Buddhism have not only been adapted over time, but how they both relate to, and support, modern scientific principles.

History of Lord Buddha

The history of Lord Buddha talks about his birth, his journey and practices, and then his death. These are important to know because by understanding the prince's background and upbringing, we can better comprehend the magnitude of his decision to seek an end to suffering, the trials he faced on his path, and how, by trial and error, he finally understood the fundamental truths that led to enlightenment.

Birth of Buddha

The birth of Buddha takes us back to 6th century BCE, to a small kingdom in India close to the Himalayan Mountains, which was ruled by King Sudhodhana of the Shakya clan. One night, his Queen, Mahamaya, had a dream where she saw a white elephant descend from heaven and enter her body from the side.

According to the Indian beliefs' system, an elephant symbolizes a number of extraordinary traits, including power, physical and mental strength, wisdom, sharp memory, exceptional mental capacity and learning ability and patience. However, not only does the elephant possess such remarkable qualities, but it is also aware that it does possess these features. Furthermore, its white colour, which symbolizes purity and peace, makes the appearance and actions of the elephant even more special.

As such, when Queen Mahamaya informed King Sudhodhana about her dream, he too sensed that this dream could not be dismissed as something trivial or merely ordinary. So, he summoned all the sages and holy men of his kingdom to interpret the Queen's dream.

All of the wise and holy men proclaimed that the dream was a clear indication that the Queen would become pregnant with a child who would be endowed with the elephant's exceptional traits, and who would grow up to become a symbol of purity and peace.

Shortly afterwards, Queen Mahamaya was indeed pregnant with her child; and, when she was full term—as per tradition—she knew she must travel to her parent's home to give birth. When she was en-route from Kapilavasthu, the capital city of her husband and King, to her parent's place with her entourage she passed an enchanting place called Lumbini. The sight of the blossoms bright, rich colours, the unadulterated air, the welcoming sounds of the chirping birds and the fragrance there had a magical effect on her. Queen Mahamaya felt so captivated by the sights and sounds there that she commanded her entourage to halt their journey and to spend some time there. No sooner did she step into the area, when she entered into labour and gave birth to a baby boy in the lap of nature itself (Lumbini would later become one of the holy places of Buddhism). The birth of this boy was both magical and mystical because, soon after his birth, instead of crying like most newborns, he took seven steps; in itself this is unheard of, but when he spoke, it was as if he was announcing to the world that a leader like none other was born.

His Journey from Prince to Enlightened One

King Sudhodhana named his son Siddhartha, which means "one who is capable of achieving his aim"; and, as predicted Siddhartha's birth was followed by abundance, prosperity and happiness throughout the kingdom.

A week after the birth of Siddhartha, his mother passed away and he was placed under the care of his mother's sister and step-mother, Mahaprajapati, who brought him up with utmost love and affection.

All the sages and wise men with whom King Sudhodhana consulted said wonderful things about the newborn Siddhartha. However, a great sage named 'Asita' on seeing the child, though willing to proclaim that Siddhartha would grow up to be a man of exceptional qualities, stopped short of declaring that he would grow up to be a great King: Siddharthas' stars showed that he would be greater, maybe even becoming a great saint who would, in later years, change the fate of millions.

The King loved his son and, determined to see him become his successor, kept him surrounded by unimaginable luxuries and prevented access to anything bad or unpleasant. Consequently, all Siddhartha experienced was beauty, health, wealth, happiness and luxury—in abundance. He was truly brought up in such a manner and style that he was deliberately shielded from even the sights, sounds, or smells of suffering and misery.

He was further trained in all disciplines and skills necessary to achieve kinghood: he studied under only the best teachers, he gained expertise in the arts of war, and he displayed the required intellect and power to make him a great king. Siddhartha's father, with an intention to push him further into this materialistic world, even married him to Yashodhara, a beautiful princess. It was soon all to change.

The Four Signs

One day, as Prince Siddhartha was travelling around his kingdom with his personal attendant, he encountered four things he had never seen before: an old man; a sick person; a corpse being transported in a funeral procession; and an ascetic who, despite living in the midst of so much of pain and suffering, appeared to be composed and full of peace, joy and compassion.

These 'four signs' left an indelible impression on both him and his mind—they changed him and his outlook towards life forever.

Suddenly, he came face to face with something from which he was kept away for such a long time, something he had never experienced before—suffering. From his attendant, he came to understand that suffering is indeed common in life and that death was inevitable for every single person who comes into this world.

So, at the age of 29, Siddhartha left his wife, his own newborn son, as well as the comfort and safety of his palace, and set out in search of truth and answers to his questions on human suffering

His quest for answers to his questions led him to join and study with two saintly gurus; but, he was left dissatisfied with their practices, sensing that they were leading him nowhere. He then left the two gurus and joined a group of five ascetics who were practicing austerities. While with the ascetics, Siddhartha practiced self-mortification for some time, but still remained clueless about the answers to his questions on suffering. So, with an even firmer intention to understand the truths of life, he decided to intensify his search efforts and stopped taking food and water.

One day, and struck by the pitiable condition of Siddhartha, a peasant girl put in front of him a bowl of sweet rice and pleaded with him to eat the food. It was at that moment that Siddhartha realized the futility of practicing austerities and extremes. Subsequently, he changed his mind and his mode of seeking answers and decided to keep away from, or avoid, all extremes. Siddhartha adopted the middle path when seeking his answers. He ate the bowl of rice that was offered, then bathed and changed into fresh clothes, following which he sat for meditation. After sitting in meditation for many days, truth eventually dawned on Siddhartha: all his questions regarding human suffering had been answered; and, on this full moon day, at the age of 35, Siddhartha became the enlightened one—The Buddha.

Death of Buddha

For about seven weeks following his enlightenment, Buddha spent his time in solitude. At the end of this period, the Buddha decided to deliver his first sermon to the five ascetics he had joined and then left, for they too were still practicing austerities while seeking and striving for the enlightened path.

So he travelled to Sarnath where, still at the age of 35, Lord Buddha delivered his first sermon to them. He continued to spread his message and word for the next 45 years. During these years he initiated thousands of believers into the Buddhist tradition, including his step-mother and aunt, Mahaprajapati; his wife, Yashodhara; his father, Sudhodhana; and his young son Rahula.

Despite his advancing age, the Buddha continued to travel to spread his word. The teachings he gave and the sermons he delivered were preparing for the next generation of Buddhist believers.

One of the Buddha's disciples, Ananda, was serving him and realized that Buddha was growing old. He said to Buddha that it was surprising how the Buddha's complexion was losing its brightness, how the Buddha's skin had become wrinkled, and how the Buddha's eyes, nose, ears, and tongue were also diminishing. Buddha replied that it was the law of nature and our body's must abide by those laws. Furthermore, he said that the law dictates that a young body is subject to aging, a healthy body at some point is subject to sickness, and a hale and hearty body is subject to death: these are realities and no-one is an exception to this law.

"I am old, worn out like a dilapidated cart held together with this straps."

"All things change. Whatever is born is subject to decay."

The Buddha wanted his disciples to realize that death was an inevitable part of life and that they should not lose sight of what their real purpose in life was. What's more, he asked them to see things as they are and not lose sight of the reality

Buddha became unwell at Kushinagara, a village in India that borders Nepal, and couldn't travel beyond that. He rested in a grove full of beautiful trees, laying down on the side with his head resting on his right hand and his left hand resting on his body. His last words to his disciples were:

"It may be that after I am gone that some of you will think, 'now we have no teacher.' But that is not how you should see it. Let the Dharma and the discipline that I have taught you be your teacher. All individual things pass away. Strive on, untiringly."

Lying in this posture, the Buddha breathed his last on a full moon day. This posture later came to be known as the Buddha's Nirvana.

Throughout his life, Buddha had been preparing his disciples to be their own teachers, teaching them about morals, discipline and doctrine. However, not once did he nominate anybody to serve as his successor or as a leader of the *sangha* (association or community). Once, Ananda, his most intimate devotee talked to him about choosing a person who would be able to succeed and lead after the Buddha had passed away; Buddha replied that he had taught Dharma to all alike and that there should not be any one person who could serve as authority to the remaining Buddhists. He then went on to say that that every Buddhist should try to be his own refuge instead of trying to seek that from an external agent.

> *"Make my teaching your light! Rely upon it;*
> *do not depend upon any other teaching. Make*
> *of yourself a light. Rely upon yourself, do not*
> *depend upon anyone else."*

The Threefold Training

One of the things which Buddha said while addressing his disciples during his last moments was to consider his teachings after he is gone, and to hold on to them steadfastly; in particular, he emphasised discipline and doctrine.

Discipline according to the Buddhist philosophy, and as described by Buddha himself, is the moral/ethical code of conduct that moulds our speech and our actions—this is what Buddhists refer to as sila, or *moral training*. Equally, Buddha also placed emphasis on doctrine—the development of man's ability to tame and control his mind. To achieve control over the mind, the doctrine comprises two components:

- cultivating concentration (Samadhi)

- developing wisdom (Panna).

This cultivation of concentration and developing wisdom are what are called *training in higher mentality* and *training in higher wisdom* respectively.

Various manifestations, or indications, of a troubled mind include jealousy, hatred, greed, ego, and ignorance. However, these manifestations can be eliminated by cultivating, developing, and perfecting our ethics, mentality and wisdom by *training in higher morality, training in higher concentration,* and *training in higher wisdom,* respectively. When adopted and carefully followed they can lead the mind to a desired tranquil state. Together, these are known as **threefold training** (or Trisikkha) and, as they are interdependent, cannot function without crossing each other's paths.

These are the principles which Buddha urges his disciples to never abandon because, when followed carefully, these ensure the passage of man to a higher level in his life (and is why the word 'higher' is attached to each of them).

These three go hand in hand because it is only when a person can straighten his ethics/morality that he will he be able to strengthen his concentration; and, it is only when he has mastered his meditation that his hunger for wisdom will be satisfied.

Training in Higher Morality

Though love and compassion serve as a foundation for *sila* (morality/moral training), it's not just about loving and having compassion for one's near and dear. No, it is only when one can make no distinction in passing their love and compassion to others not related to them, will there be a success of morality. Moreover, only when one loves everybody as if they were his own will they not think of doing anything that can either hurt, or cause pain and suffering

Training in moral conduct or morality involves 3 essential elements: *right speech, right action,* and *right livelihood.*

Right Speech

Right speech deals with using the right words, the right language, communicating appropriately, always speaking the truth, being fearless about speaking the truth, and being fearless about accepting and embracing the truth.

Naturally, to be able to speak, face and accept the truth requires an element of will power and mental strength to face the backlash. Yet, possessing the will to adhere to what is right will engender the needed strength to go on to lead an ethical and moral life.

Right speech also refers to abstaining from talking ill of others to either spoil their reputation, tarnish their image, assassinate their character, develop hatred, or create a rift between people. Let's be clear, right speech means not disturbing the harmony and tranquillity of somebody's mind with one's own talk; it is about avoiding making the minds of others restless and agitated (as evidenced when seeking revenge). Furthermore, right speech is also about refraining from speaking ill of others without any basis, of jealousy, and to do so with the sole intention of creating a negative perception of them in the view of others.

Right speech is about not engaging in a rude, rash, and impolite talk or discussion that could hurt the feelings of others.

Right speech is about speaking after a lot of thinking, contemplation, and consideration. Right speech is never about using profane language that could in any way disturb the mind of the person using it and at whom it is targeted.

Right speech is about adopting language and tone that is genuinely pleasant, friendly, filled with warmth, love, affection, concern, compassion, that is sensible, and is unpretentious.

Right speech requires one to speak only when required and to utter only what is essential and where it is necessary. Finally, right speech implies that if one does not have anything worthy of saying or the time is inopportune then the noblest thing to do would be to maintain silence.

Of course, before one can determine the right speech in any given situation, it is important to first appreciate and understand the right action.

Right Action

Right action is about knowing and choosing the correct decision in any given situation. What's more, it's about taking the correct decisions with integrity, and choosing what is right irrespective of how hard and difficult the path is to traverse. It is also about having and maintaining a firm conviction to both make the right decision and to achieve that action without wavering.

In addition, right action also refers to selecting and heading off on the honourable path no matter how difficult it actually is or how many hardships you are forced to face. It is also concerned with not engaging in actions that could disrupt the lives of others, be they humans or animals (whether hunting or not), and cheating people.

Simply put, if pleasure can only be derived at the cost of others then it is not the right action.

Right Livelihood

Right livelihood deals with confining oneself only to those activities and professions which are legal and do good to humanity. Similarly, right livelihood refers to avoiding activities which could cause suffering or endanger people, animals, or the environment, including rejecting professions or activities that are illegal, such as human trafficking, kidnapping, murder, or dealing in drugs and substances

Additionally, right livelihood is about refraining from making a living by doing business and things that could prove harmful to others. These include: dealing in arms, weapons, ammunition, making destructive material, dealing in drugs and alcohol, human trafficking, engaging underage children in work, robbery, thefts, murder and kidnapping.

To summarise *Training in Higher Morality,* Buddha teaches us that practicing virtue in our speech, in conducting ourselves in the way we approach and do things, and in living correctly enables us to live both morally and ethically; and, without these our journey for a meaningful life, and ultimate spirituality will end even before it has begun.

Buddha always said that it is better to die rather than to break our ethics and morals because death brings an end to just one life, but breaking our morals will affect our karma and could set us back several lives and destroy our opportunity to experience happiness in this life and in many lives to come.

Training in Higher Mentality

As was mentioned, morality can be strengthened by reigning in our speech, our actions, and the way we lead our daily lives; unfortunately, though these are indeed steps in the right direction, more is required.

You see, it's quite possible that a person may not say anything wrong or bad, and they may not do anything that is offensive, obnoxious, or bad, but that doesn't mean the person is pure in their thoughts; and, this is where training in mentality comes into play. If a person's speech sounds enchanting, and their visual display is appealing, it may mask what is beneath the surface— their inner thoughts oppose their outward display. However, if their thoughts are aligned with their pure persona, then naturally the outcome will be purity in mind, as well as speech and actions. Likewise, if the source itself is bad then the outcome can be corrupt or contaminated; so, it is essential to be trained in focussing our mental state/concentration.

Training in mentality refers to not only developing the right thoughts, but also keeping the right thoughts alive all the time, as well as keeping the negative thoughts at bay. To be precise, the three components that comprise training in higher mentality are: *right effort*, *right mindfulness*, and *right concentration.*

Right Effort

Right effort is required to keep the bad, unsavoury, or unhealthy thoughts under control. It is important to instil effort and exert oneself to prevent the above thoughts entering the mind. As we all know, bad thoughts do crop up, so right effort also involves nipping them in the bud when they do arise, as well as improving one's own store of good thoughts: putting a determined effort in maximising the store of good thoughts and minimising the store of bad ones is both a helpful and good practice.

Right Mindfulness

Being constantly on the guard to watch for any disturbing, distracting thoughts trying to find a place in the mind. Right mindfulness plays a prominent role in furthering one's spiritual progress.

Right mindfulness and Right effort together lead to the next essential component in Mentality which is Right concentration

Right Concentration

The purpose of concentration is to remain unperturbed, unfazed, and unbothered in all scenarios, circumstances, and conditions. Your focus needs to be on spiritual enhancement and progress and to try not to let anything come in their way. As you may realise, it's common for people who are experiencing suffering to be spiritually inclined and to develop indifference for everything; yet, when the situation is good they quickly reengage with their materialistic pursuits again putting their spiritual journey and well-being firmly behind them. However, when one is focused on a spiritual path then both good and bad times alike are treated equally and the person appears indifferent to the circumstances.

To summarise, regardless of circumstances, a focused person is happy, joyous, peaceful, calm and composed.

Training in Higher Wisdom

No matter how much a person has read, how good their learning capacity is, how intelligent they are, how good they are at talking, how sweet their words are, how much knowledge they have acquired, how much others look up to them for their erudition and learning, they are not a person of wisdom if they are bothered by disturbing, disrupting and distracting thoughts. Only a person who has reigned in their thoughts (a situation where a person controls their thoughts and their thoughts do not control them) is a person of wisdom. Buddha said that only a fool will consider them-self most intelligent and learned and yet fall prey to their own disrupting thoughts.

Right Understanding

True wisdom is about being able to differentiate and understand what is real, what gives real happiness, and what provides permanent joy. It is also about developing an insight into the simple truths of life and conducting oneself accordingly.

Right Thoughts

Correct thoughts that do not stem from negative feelings and emotions, such as jealousy, hatred and anger, form the basis for wisdom. Ultimately, a person's essential aim should be their spiritual progress and enlightenment, and whatever is either not helping or hindering them in their spiritual pursuit should be filtered and thrown out.

People can be learned and intelligent but if they are not using that intelligence wisely, perhaps only to eat and sleep well, to settle scores with their enemies, to make more enemies, etc., then having those attributes is of little use.

To close this training section, wisdom is the one faculty that differentiates us from animals, but if it either remains unused or is used incorrectly, then it is simply wasted. It should be used to expedite kindness to all, to generate and spread love and compassion, and to discover how to end suffering, both for oneself and for others.

The Principles of Buddhism and Principles of Science

> *"Buddhism is not a collection of views. It is a practice to help us eliminate wrong views."*

Thich Nhat Hanh, The Heart of Buddha's Teaching

As I will show shortly, there are a number of similarities between the principles of Buddhism and the principles of Science, but a key element to appreciate is that Buddhism is very adaptive. Indeed, as the Dalai Lama said, *"If scientific analysis were conclusively to demonstrate certain claims in Buddhism to be false, then we must accept the findings of science and abandon those claims."* (Lama, The Universe in a Single Atom: The Convergence of Science and Spirituality, 2006). As such, as the world evolves, and new findings are unearthed, then Buddhism must also adapt to this new knowledge. The following shows 10 areas where similarities exist:

1. **Impossible to Fail:** Science requires insight, reasoning, and effort (or perseverance). As you may already realise, there is no place for failure in science, because not finding success in an experiment or investigation cannot be termed failure it's just proof that this particular process does not work in favour of the experiment. So, without getting disheartened and armed with new hope, new vigour, new methodologies, and new hypotheses, scientists move on to testing for success in what they are trying to do, be it trying to invent something, discover, or prove.

    Similarly, Siddhartha did not know what the results would be when he first started his journey on the spiritual path; but, he persisted. In the same way as scientists explore, he was curious, inquisitive, thirsty for knowledge, and hungry for finding the solutions to his questions. However, he was not worried about the time frame, and he was not concerned about getting quick results, rather seeking an everlasting solution. During his quest, he did not hesitate to experiment and 'fail'; but, more importantly, his determination was intact, and he did not quit. With each 'setback', he modified his methodology and finally, after 6 long years, he attained enlightenment – he proved his theory.

2. **Inner Potential:** As the science fraternity believes, science holds key to endless discoveries, inventions, innovations and possibilities. What is required to unlock these advancements is an analytical bent of mind, an investigative nature, and perseverance. Accordingly, they believe and support their inner strength rather than reliance on any external agent.

    Buddha too believed that there is an immense potential lying latent in every person, and all that is required to tap that intrinsic potential is not divine intervention, but the belief in oneself.

3. **Verification:** One of the foundations of science is verification, the ability to repeat and confirm results. To be able to verify results, science needs data, research, hypothesis, experimentation, and evidence—it requires proof; and, without this nothing can be interpreted or deduced. Every individual experiment is unique, which gives rise to unique experiences for the people involved in it; and, due to the differing perspectives of individuals, scientists must record their results based on their observations and not on the observations of others.

    Buddha also asked his disciples not to take him as a final authority. He taught them to believe and to follow something only after they have themselves tested and verified it. He asked them to pay attention to their experiences rather than to what others have experienced or said. He said:

"Do not accept things just because I your teacher have said so. Be your own teacher."

"Monks and scholars should well analyse my words, like gold to be tested through melting, cutting and polishing. Only then should they adopt them, but not for the sake of showing me respect."

Buddhism encourages its believers (or those interested in Buddhism) to see for themselves, to test for themselves rather than relying on the observations of others. Furthermore, relying on one's own experiences enables you to absorb and follow something (principles and doctrines) because you yourself believe in it. As you yourself have tested it, you therefore find it readily acceptable...much in the same way as science talks about reasoning, gaining insight, hypotheses, testing, experimenting and validating

"Do not go upon what has been acquired by repeated hearing; nor upon tradition; nor upon rumor; nor upon what is in a scripture; nor upon surmise; nor upon an axiom; nor upon specious reasoning; nor upon a bias towards a notion that has not been pondered over; nor upon another's seeming ability; nor upon the consideration, 'The monk is our teacher.' Rather, when you yourselves know that these things are good; these things are not blamable; undertaken and observed, these things lead to benefit and happiness, then and only then enter into and abide in them."

4. **The Universe:** Science has proven that there is a universe that is made up of planets, stars, galaxies and more.

   According to Buddhism, there exists not just one world with one sun, one moon and one earth, but there are thousands of suns, moons and earths that are present in a thousand worlds.

5. **Cause and Effect:** Both Science and Buddhism believe in the law of causality, i.e., the principle of cause and effect: something causes an event to occur, and this triggers something else to happen.

6. **No place for Superstition:** In Science there is no place for superstitious beliefs. Anything that cannot be proved, and for which evidence cannot be provided, is unfounded.

   Buddha also did away with superstitious beliefs, rituals and customs that either made no sense, which he could not relate to, or which he thought were mere adornment and cannot assist in the attainment of liberation and enlightenment.

7. **Flexibility:** Neither Science nor Buddhism are rigid, nor both have a very flexible approach. Even if a new finding disapproves of or contradicts an earlier experiment, methodology, result or conclusion, it is still accepted.

   It is much the same with Buddhism. If something contradictory to a common or accepted belief is proved then Buddhism does not hesitate to test that new idea or study, in order to understand and accept it. Anything that has been scientifically proven is acceptable in

Buddhism; and, as was mentioned earlier, Buddhism must adapt itself to new theories.

For example, centuries ago, when the common agreement was that the earth was flat and the sun revolved around the earth, Buddhists believed also; yet, when Science proved these false, Buddhists did not hesitate to change their belief.

8. **Impermanence:** Science believes in impermanence. We are all aware that change is perpetual: nature is evolving, the seasons are changing, the universe is expanding, and ultimately, on a human level, we change too—nothing is ever static, everything is in motion.

Buddhism also believes in this concept, that everybody and everything is bound to change: a child will grow into an adult, and an adult will grow old; a person who is born will not live forever; a healthy person will not retain his health forever, and so forth. Nothing is permanent, and everything will change.

9. **The Principle of Mass**: In Science, one definition of mass is the property of a physical body which determines its strength of mutual gravitational attraction on other bodies: the greater the mass of the body, the more it gets attracted to other bodies; and, as part of this process it loses some of its own energy. Also, as energy can be exchanged between particles, those with a lesser mass can draw energy more quickly.

In the same manner as Science talks about mass (and the way it is intertwined with energy), Buddhism talks about ignorance. Ignorance is something which misleads us into thinking that happiness is derived from materials, people and other transient or impermanent things...the more ignorance (or things) we have and cling onto, the greater are our suffering if they are lost; moreover, this also decrease our own chances of salvation or enlightenment.

Where Science talks about energy, Buddhism talks about happiness: we gain energy when we are happy (we attract) and we lose energy when we are sad (we repel). So, when a person is happy they attract and draw energy much quicker than when they are sad (have you noticed how happy people attract similar?) Of course, if we minimise or remove the chances or causes of our sadness, then we will naturally absorb more happiness/energy.

10. **Attraction:** An electric field creates a magnetic field, and vice versa (electromagnetism). In the same way these fields affect the objects around them, by either attracting or pushing them away, Buddhist principles say that our surroundings cause happiness and when happy the value of the surroundings also increases. As mentioned above, happy people attract similar, and sad people are often lonely. However, it must be said, that there is no one single source of happiness, rather there are multiple 'fields'; and, in the same way as electromagnetic fields affect different objects in different ways, different sources of happiness have different levels of attraction.

Another by-product of electric and magnetic fields is light. In this particular combination, a wave can be produced carries energy in the form of light that is radiated out.

As I'm sure you have experienced, kindness and compassion can also be radiated, producing happiness around you, as well as generating greater kindness and compassion, much in the way of a light -wave of spiritual energy.

Now we have looked at the Principles of Buddhism and Science, and seen how they align, let's quickly look at the Buddhist beliefs.

Buddhist Beliefs

There are a number of Buddhist beliefs, but here are the 5 main ones:

1. Buddha is not a God.

    This is key to understanding Buddhism. Buddha neither is, nor was a God. Also, neither was he a messenger of God nor a prophet. Buddha was born an ordinary human being who set out on a path to perfect himself. He strived hard to develop kindness, compassion and peace in his believers; and, he taught and showed us that it is not impossible to overcome suffering in our lives.

    Worship to Buddha is not formal. If Buddhists fold their hands or bow in front of a Buddha's statue, it is to express their gratitude and respect to him for his teachings. When they use flowers, it is to remind themselves that nothing in this world is permanent and, like flowers, everything will wilt. If they use a lamp, or candles, then this helps to remind themselves about the power of truth and knowledge.

2. We have a purpose in life.

   Buddhists believe that they are all driven by a common purpose, to end suffering in their lives.

3. There is an afterlife that depends on the present life.

   All our actions, be they good or bad, have consequences—karma. Our good actions will create a good store of merits—good karma—and our bad actions will create a bad store of merits—bad karma. Furthermore, until one attains enlightenment, life continues through rebirth and the consequences of our actions in the present life can be felt and seen in our next life. Every Buddhist should strive to end his cycle of rebirth—enlightenment or nirvana.

4. Meditation is essential to stay connected with your mind.

   There are many benefits that are associated with meditating regularly. Meditation gives us the opportunity to look deep into ourselves, which enables us to cleanse our mind, to straighten our speech, to ponder right actions and right thoughts, as well as improving our ability to focus and concentrate.

5. Staying associated with the spiritual community is important.

   The spiritual community serves as a guiding force and a source of motivation; and is a place where like-minded people with similar objectives come together. The positive energy created in such places is so potent that it creates a much greater impact than reading scriptures and books alone.

"Life can be found only in the present moment. The past is gone, the future is not yet here, and if we do not go back to ourselves in the present moment, we cannot be in touch with life."

Thich Nhat Hanh

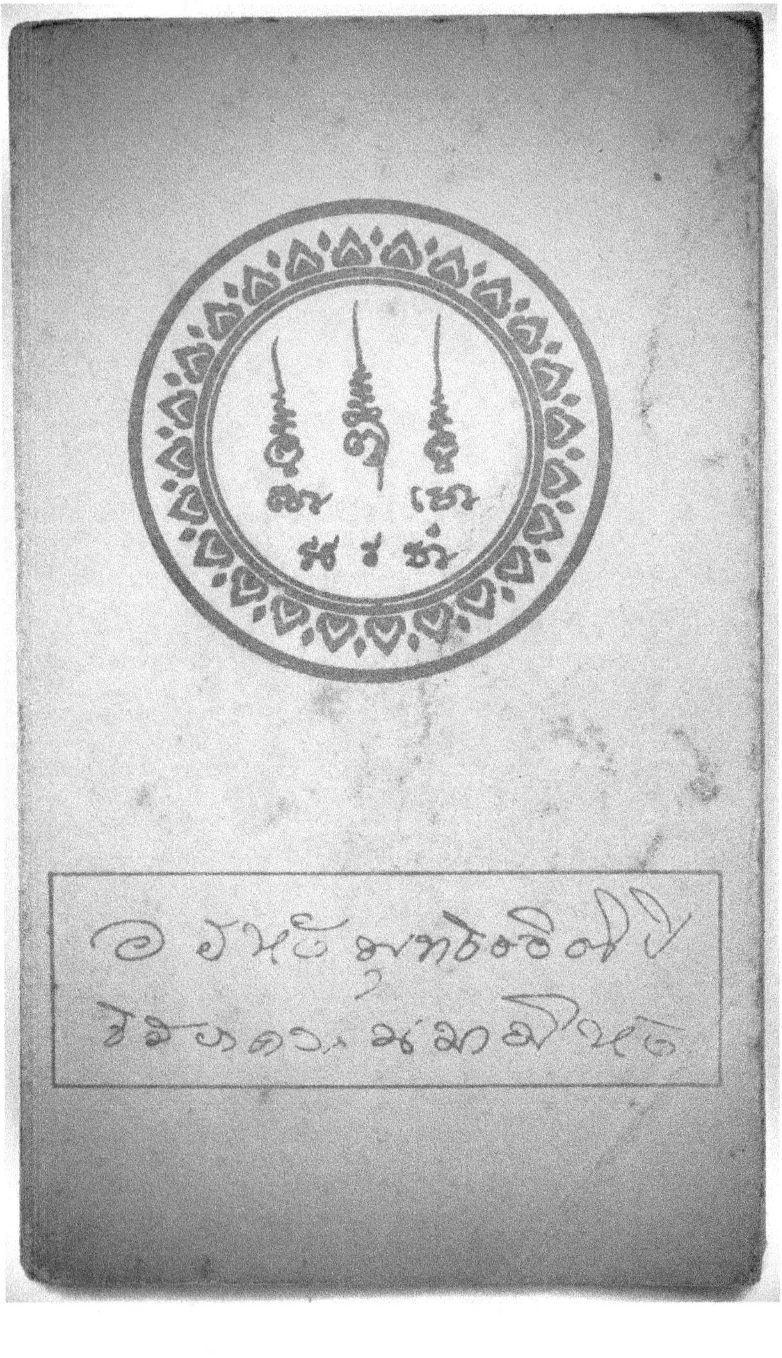

Chapter 2. Buddhist Teaching Guides

The Triple Gems of Buddhism

The triple gems of Buddhism are also called as the three jewels, three treasures, three refuges, precious triad, or *Triratna* in Sanskrit.

When a person decides to become a Buddhist, the first thing they will do is to seek refuge in the three gems: Buddha, Dharma, and Sangha. They do this by stating:

I take refuge in Buddha

I take refuge in Dharma

I take refuge in Sangha.

To proclaim devotion to the three gems is to be a Buddhist. It may help to think of this like a process where a person is first initiated into Buddhism, and is where they subsequently go to get to know and to understand the historical Buddha: the Triple Gems (Buddha, Dharma, and Sangha) show the way to end suffering.

When a Buddhist believer is at this early initiation stage, they are bound more by inquisitiveness and an inquiring mode. However, it is an important step, as it is only after the person understands who Buddha is, and what the three gems actually are— how one can seek refuge, how the three gems can save a person from the misery and suffering prevalent all around—do they choose, or make the decision, to become a Buddhist. Again, it may help to think of this like an initiation into the order.

The three gems are the ideals that form the **heart of Buddhism**; and they are the principles that seek to satisfy the inquisitiveness of those who come to understand Buddha and how they can be saved from misery and suffering.

Buddha

Buddha here doesn't merely signify the founder of Buddhism/ historical Buddha. Here Buddha signifies both the enlightened Buddha as well as the centrality revolving around the idea of Buddha.

Buddha is considered to be the epitome of wisdom and a truly enlightened person. So, when a Buddhist professes to take refuge in Buddha, they mean that there is nothing better than to be enlightened and that there is nothing safer than seeking refuge in the most enlightened person. It's tantamount to taking an oath that *"I seek refuge in enlightenment to ensure my safety and security."* Indeed, going to Buddha to seek refuge is like going to the ultimate teacher to seek answers to all our questions...and is the very first step on the path to enlightenment.

The second step is the Dharma.

Dharma

Dharma, meaning 'truth' in Sanskrit, is the second gem (or the second jewel) of Triratna. Dharma is symbolized by the wheel.

The *Dharma* contains the teachings of Buddha. These teachings are based on the four *Noble Truths* which create a strong foundation for Buddhism.

The *Dharma* also emphasizes that a person is sure to be freed from the clutches of ignorance only when the 4 noble truths (that are mentioned in the Dharma) are practiced regularly. Only then can the person seek refuge in the Dharma (seeking refuge is like saying that I am safe and secure now that I have taken this refuge). As you can see, the Dharma can only protect you if your path to the truth is begun with a serious and definite intention: seeking refuge in the Dharma is seeking guidance from Buddha through his teachings, and agreeing to follow them is with a firm conviction that you will tread this path to become enlightened.

In conclusion, Dharma is about cleansing, purifying and conditioning one's mind, instilling compassion, kindness, love and ethical values.

Sangha

The *Sangha* refers to the community of monks (bhikkhus), nuns (bhikkhunis), and lay followers (male and female) who are practicing the Dharma.

The sangha shoulders the responsibility of spreading the message of Buddha out of compassion for mankind, and is guided by a strong intent to put those who believe in Buddhism on the path to enlightenment. Sangha can also include teachers who are ahead of us on the path to enlightenment and are willing to be the guiding lights that will dispel the surrounding darkness on our quest for truth. As we all know, it is helpful to have teachers to guide us and to help us as we traverse the path of dharma.

The sangha is meant to convey to others that the path of the Dharma—the path to attain enlightenment—can indeed be treaded and progress can always be made to achieve enlightenment.

The Foundational Doctrines of Buddhism

After attaining enlightenment, Buddha gave his first sermon in deer park in a place called Sarnath. This first sermon was on the four Noble Truths, which not only form the basis of Buddhism, but also hold the essence of the teachings of the Buddha

The four noble truths are as follows:

1. The truth of suffering

2. The truth of the cause of suffering

3. The truth of freedom from suffering

4. The truth of the path that leads to cessation of (freedom from) suffering

The Buddha's exposition on the four noble truths mainly focusses on ways to alleviate and to finally end the suffering which he had witnessed and experienced. His quest for an answer to the question of suffering began with him first identifying that suffering is common in life and prevalent across all cultures, regardless of wealth, health, status, or age.

The Truth of Suffering

The first truth says that suffering is present all the time and is conspicuous.

Suffering pervades through every stage of life, be it birth, death, adulthood, or old age, and it can manifest in both physical and mental forms.

Physical Suffering

Physical suffering can be caused by disease, pain, injury, sickness or age-related problems. One may be hale and hearty, but as everything is impermanent, this is only for a brief period of time. As we know, the only thing constant in this life is change: a young person will grow old, a person with youthful looks will one day lose all their charm, a healthy person will eventually lose that good health and vigour, it is a matter of time. Consequently, as the Buddha says, a person cannot be thoroughly happy even if they are enjoying good health, good looks, and in their youth, because the fear of losing these one day causes suffering.

Mental suffering

As we all know, suffering does not manifest itself in the physical form alone, it can also affect us mentally in many ways, including: sadness, depression, feelings of rejection and dejection, anger, stress, jealousy, hatred, loneliness and hopelessness. All these example are mental manifestations of suffering. It is a fact of life that we experience different levels of sadness, depending on our individual relationships and circumstances; for example, being sad about the death of a loved one, angry with someone close to us, becoming dejected about not getting what we want and desire, or even resenting or being jealous about someone achieving something we wanted ourselves—all these are mental suffering.

When Buddha spoke about suffering he did not deny that happiness is also part of life. Happiness arising out of relationships, friendships, progress in life, achievements in life, the love and respect one gets in life, and so on are all good examples; but, they too are impermanent. When happiness is gone, it again leads to sadness and suffering.

Of course, each of us is happy to be with those we love, but when it's time for them to leave, our happiness is lost leaving both an emptiness and a desperate desire for more time with your loved one—you suffer.

For material objects, such as a car. You are happy you bought the car, you feel a sense of pride in what you have, but if the car gets damaged in an accident, again you suffer.

So, the Buddha's first noble truth asks the people to identify and accept that nobody is devoid of suffering, it is common to us all, and is an integral part of life.

The Truth of the Cause of Suffering

Buddha's second noble truth says that suffering is primarily caused by ignorance and desire. They are the root causes of suffering and misery in everyone's life.

The desire for materialistic pleasures, power, fame, comforts, a healthy life without death, a life without worries, a life of abundance, desire to be above all and above everything are just few of the many yearnings we have. Unfortunately, the cycle is never-ending and the end of one desire frequently leads to the birth of another desire, and on-and-on—there are no ends to our desires. In fact, these desires, these cravings for more and more, can lead to so much of unhappiness, and discontent in our lives, that it triggers negative feelings, emotions and reactions, and agitates and robs the mind of its peace, thereby causing suffering. Again, none of the things we long for provide lasting happiness

For example, a beautiful person might desire to remain beautiful forever because being beautiful makes her very happy; but it will not last—it cannot last—because nothing is permanent. So their fading beauty causes them suffering. Sure, you can use technology to try and maintain your body and youthful look, you can go under the knife to make sure you remain beautiful, but at what price? There is the knowledge that this may be just one in a series of procedures, each more risky than the last—suffering; there may be side effects to this—suffering. So attempting to associate happiness with temporary pleasures will never ensure lasting happiness.

Ignorance, is another root cause of suffering: our inability to see reality, inability to gain insight of the reality, inability to accept the hard truths of life, inability to let the things pass as per their nature, ignorance in trying to understand the impermanent nature of life, and inability to understand the true nature of things, all leads to the same thing.

Ignorance sows seeds for desire to flourish

When the mind is controlled by desire and ignorance, it becomes so clouded that it loses the ability to think, reason and rationalise thereby triggering negative feelings, emotions, reactions, behaviours, thoughts, such as envy, jealousy, hatred, greed, avarice, or worse.

The Truth of Freedom from Suffering

The 3rd noble truth emphasizes that suffering does not have to be prevalent in one's life; it emphasises that it is possible to end that suffering.

Buddha said that suffering could be ended by getting rid of desire and ignorance. Doing so gives way to compassion and where there is compassion, there is peace and joy all around. Moreover, a person who is compassionate will not hesitate to help others seek liberation from suffering. The reality to this is that when ignorance dies, one become a person of wisdom and deep insight. Such a person sees things as they truly are and will not be affected by changes in personal circumstances, treating what would be considered both happy and sad circumstances alike.

The Truth of the Path that Leads to Cessation of Suffering

The fourth noble truth talks about the methods that should be adopted to ensure an ending to suffering in our lives. This method is called the noble *eightfold path*. The Buddha laid down eight steps for a person to practice, so that he could bring his sufferings and misery to an end and proceed on the path to enlightenment.

The Eightfold Path

We have two extremes at the opposite ends of the scale: one is over-indulgence in materialistic comforts and pleasures, which undoubtedly leads to greater desires; the other is practicing asceticism and self-mortification in the name of giving up everything. Unfortunately, both extremes actually involve more suffering and pain and are actually futile in removing suffering. Because of this, Buddha proposed that we should adopt the *middle path*; he called it the eightfold path. This eightfold path aims at developing morality, mentality and wisdom; and, as it is more effective when put to use in every aspect of life, should be practiced daily.

Doing so, is a simple yet powerful approach and will have a deep impact on a person with respect to their approach towards life. The eightfold path is as follows:

1. Right understanding

2. Right thought

3. Right speech

4. Right action

5. Right livelihood

6. Right effort

7. Right mindfulness

8. Right concentration

Following these simple yet powerful steps ensures peace, calm, knowledge, insight, enlightenment and, finally, nirvana.

We have already discussed of these before, and as we know the 2 steps of **right understanding**, and **right thought**, make up the components of good wisdom.

Developing wisdom is about encouraging the right thoughts and fostering deeper insight and understanding to help us differentiate between right and wrong, good and bad, and what should be avoided and welcomed. Wisdom is about developing a firm conviction to remain fixed on the path of truth and to see things as they really are.

Right Understanding involves going above superficial understanding and gaining deep insight. Everyone is aware that suffering is common in life, but rarely does anyone really bother to understand the causes of that suffering, and even fewer seek how they could actually put an end to their suffering. Right understanding is about understanding the real truths of life—one's purpose in life, almost. As you can see, here, we're talking about going beyond the books, scriptures and texts to obtain a deeper understanding of the true essence of life.

Right thought directs that our speech, action and decision-making should be directed by the way that we think. There is no synchronization if our thoughts say one thing and our speech/actions says another. As we have all probably experienced, speech and actions can both sound and appear virtuous, but if they originate from an unvirtuous thought, then that speech or those actions cannot be associated with wisdom. It is only if the speech or action stems from a right thought will it be genuine and pure.

The 3 steps of **right speech**, **right action**, and **right livelihood** make up the components of good conduct/morality.

To reiterate, wrong speech gives rise to lies, deceit, ill-feelings, hatred, anger, stress, tension, rift between people/groups, assassination of somebody's character and reputation. But right speech creates harmony, happiness, compassion, kindness and cordial atmosphere.

Wrong actions will harm people, society, or the environment, so should be avoided. Whereas right actions are helpful to everyone and everything.

Similarly, the wrong livelihood will cause harm and suffering to those around us; and this includes butchering, gambling, human trafficking, trading in weapons, drugs, etc. On the other hand, choosing to earn a living in a peaceful, acceptable, and productive way that can benefit you as well as the society is the desired choice. Surely the welfare and progress of all should be paramount in our choice of preferred livelihood?

The 3 steps of *right effort*, *right mindfulness*, and *right concentration* make up the components of good mentality.

Right effort involves:

- Preventing evil, disturbing and distracting thoughts from arising in the mind.

- Cleansing the mind of the existing unwanted thoughts.

- Causing good, healthy and productive thoughts to arise in the mind.

- Improving the presence of already prevalent wholesome thoughts in the mind.

Right mindfulness is about being alert and attentive to the thoughts that come and go out of the mind, being totally aware of the feelings and emotions associated with the thoughts.

Right concentration is about being focused on attaining the ultimate goal.

To summarise, the eightfold path is a systematic and stepped approach to ridding oneself of suffering and progressing one's own path to achieving enlightenment.

The Five Precepts for Living

Buddhism discourages its followers from using any action, speech or behaviour that could prove harmful to oneself, to others, or to society. The Buddhist tradition has also been built in such a manner that it encourages a person to develop a skilled mind. Doing so ensures that the person is equipped to decide or act in a manner that will not be regretful.

The five precepts for living are no different, and they leave ample scope for a person to put their skilled mind to use.

The five precepts are not rules, regulations, or commandments which, if broken, would entail punishment in a severe form. Rather, they are basic training principles, or rules, which help those preparing to become Buddhists to develop a skilled mind. Since Buddhism lays so much emphasis on the mind, the breaking of any of the rules should also be governed by the mind. It is essential that those who wish to tread the path to enlightenment have a mind that is free of guilt, regret and remorse; thereby, any decisions or actions they subsequently take will leave that person guilt free. If there is a breach, the mind should be aware of it so that remedial actions can be taken and the action would not again be repeated.

Being a flexible tradition, the Buddhist order acknowledges that several views, or angles, may be necessary to approach or understand any given situation, behaviour, or problem. Accordingly, Buddhism does not impose rigid and strict rules with respect to any course of action which one is supposed to take in a particular situation. So, instead of listing the right and wrong actions, or those that are forbidden in the Buddhist tradition, the tradition has laid out certain principles.

Since these principles are concerned with ethics, it is important to use a logical amount of sensitivity when such situations are encountered:

1.   To abstain from taking the life of a living being.

This is the most important ethical principle in Buddhism as every living being has a right to live; and Buddhism tells its followers to respect that right. Based on compassion, kindness and love, this precept discourages a Buddhist from being violent.

2.   To abstain from taking what is not given or stealing.

Stealing is one way to cause harm to others, and by stealing you are depriving a person of what is rightfully theirs. The underlying basis of this precept is generosity.

3.   To abstain from sexual misconduct.

Legal and emotional issues aside, sexual misconduct can have serious implications that include causing harm to oneself or to others, causing damage to one's reputation, breaking or misusing the commitment made to a person, and many more consequences. So this precept indicates that not only should one abstain from committing such mistake but also to discourage others from doing so to. The underlying basis of this precept is propriety.

Misconduct in this sense, can also mean abstaining from any sensual pleasure such as overeating.

4.   To abstain from using harsh speech and telling lies.

Speech plays a very important role in our lives and, as such, should be used to speak the truth, and to produce gentle, encouraging and comforting words. But, sadly, speech is too often misused. This precept prevents people from lying and hurting others and is based on truthfulness.

5.   To abstain from intoxicants or harmful substances.

Intoxicating drinks and drugs cloud the mind of the person consuming them. They can also diminish the judgement-taking capacity of the person and, when the person's mind is blurry, they cannot be alert and attentive.

Intoxicants can blur our judgement which can also impact the other four precepts because, in an intoxicated or inebriated condition, a person can lose control and break the training rules.

The Three Baskets of Buddha's Teachings

The word of Buddha consists of 3 aspects: doctrine, practice, and realization. It is the doctrine that makes the three baskets of Buddha's teachings. These three baskets contain Buddha's teachings, sermons, and discourses, starting with the first sermon (delivered in the deer park at Sarnath after his enlightenment) till his death, 45 years later.

The three baskets are called Tripitaka in Sanskrit. They form the basic scriptures which capture the essence of Buddhism:

- **Vinaya** – talks about the appropriate ways to behave.

- **Sutta** – what kind of thoughts to embrace and what kind of thoughts to abandon.

- **Abhidhamma** – touches upon the important and higher aspects of Buddhism and its teachings.

Origins

These teachings were written down almost 500 years after Buddha's death. Prior to that, the teachings were memorized and taught orally. When the teachings were first written down, it was onto long narrow leaves which were then sewn together and tied into bunches; these were then placed into separate baskets—hence the name 'three baskets'.

The three baskets also signify the passing down of the baskets from one generation to another generation of believers, from teacher to a believer. Each basket plays a unique role in the Buddhist tradition.

The Discipline Basket

The **discipline basket** (*Vinaya Pitaka*) because it lays down rules and regulations intended for monks and nuns at the sangha (the community of monks and nuns).

The rules and regulations laid out for the monks and nuns include details about the permitted level and form of interaction between monks and nuns, how to dress, as well as details pertaining to robe-making and other basic but essential information to help them lead a productive life at the sangha.

As was mentioned in the section about the Principles of Buddhism and Science, Buddhism is flexible and Vinaya Pitaka talks about how breaking a rule under certain conditions is not considered breach of conduct. For example, though monks are not supposed to partake of any food after noon, if they are unwell and have to eat something after midday to aid their recovery, then the rule is not considered broken.

The Discourse Basket

As the name suggests, the **discourse basket** (*Sutta Pitaka*) and, as the name itself suggests, is a collection of the discourses and sermons of Buddha, as well as transcripts of discussion and conversation which Buddha had with the monks and nuns of the Buddhist tradition. This basket aims at improving a person's thought processes, thereby helping him both welcome good thoughts and abandon disturbing thoughts.

Sutta Pitaka also has a collection of stories of past births and lives of Buddha known as Jatakas. Finally, also included in this basket is one of the most important texts, the *Dhammapada*, (Buddha's exposition on law), which comprises 423 verses containing important instructions to Buddhist believers.

Life Lessons

The life lessons (*Abhidhamma Pitaka*) are a collection of texts that clarify on subjects concerning time, matter, and mind. Altogether, the scriptures have great significance in the Buddhist tradition because they provide valuable information about how to lead one's life.

*Sometimes your joy is the source of your smile,
but sometimes your smile can be the source of
your joy.*

Thich Nhat Hanh

Chapter 3. Sacred Activities

I n this section we will look at the Buddhist holy days, festivals, and ceremonies.

Buddhist Holy Days

There are 4 main Buddhist holy days in a calendar year: Magha Puja, Visakha Puja, Atthame Puja, and Asalha Puja. We will look at each in turn, as well as other holy days.

Magha Puja

During the time of the Buddha, 1250 of his disciples, those who had followed in his footsteps to attain enlightenment, all came to him to pay their respects. This particular day was the first full moon day of Magha and, for this very reason, this day is observed on the first full day of every Magha (March), the 3rd lunar month in the Indian calendar.

The day is also called Sangha day in order to remember the 1250 monks who belonged to the monastic sangha. Another name

you may hear Magha Puja being referred to is the 'Fourfold Assembly Day', for the following reasons:

1. All the 1250 monks were arahants (this means they were enlightened ones all of whom attained Nirvana)

2. All of them were initiated into the Buddhist tradition by Buddha himself.

3. The coming together of all the 1250 monks was unplanned and simply a matter of coincidence.

4. This event took place on the first full moon day of Magha.

Buddha delivered a sermon to the 1250 monks gathered there, and talked about good and bad actions as well as about ways to keep the mind purified. Lay-people commemorate this day by visiting temples and circumnavigating the chapel or a statue of Buddha while holding 1 bunch of flowers, 3 incense sticks, and 1 candle in their hands as a sign of respect for Buddha, Dharma and Sangha; they also offer food and other items to the monks in the sangha.

Visakha Puja Day

Visakha Puja day is also known as the Buddha Day and is celebrated on the first full moon day of May (except in a leap year when it is celebrated in the month of June).

This is considered a very special and holy day by Buddhists all over the world. On this day they celebrate the birth of Buddha, 2500 years ago, his enlightenment, and also remember his departure from this world.

Atthame Puja Day

Atthame Puja Day occurs on the 8th day of the waning moon of the 6th or 7th lunar month. This day occurs seven days after Visakha Puja Day and commemorates the day on which the body of Buddha was cremated. The ceremony is hosted at the temple and most of the participants are monks. The day is to remind Buddhists to behave and believe in good karma, to live their lives carefully, and to be aware that the body is impermanent: birth, old age, injury, and death are a part of life, and no one can escape them.

Asalha Puja Day

This day is also called Dharma Day and is celebrated on a full moon day sometime in July, the 8th lunar month. This day commemorates the first sermon of the Buddha to his first five disciples in the deer park at Sarnath, India.

Typically, on any special or holy day, Buddhists go to the temple, circumnavigate the chapel three times, take the five precepts, listen to discourses on Buddha's teachings and the life of Buddha, and participate in meditation and chanting along with fellow Buddhists.

Other Buddhist Holy Days

As I've just shown, there are 4 main holy days each year, but there are other, minor, Buddhist holy days (or *Thammasawana*) which occur four times a month with the following moon phases:

1. The 8th day of the waxing moon

2. The 15th day of the waxing moon (the full moon)

3. The 8th day of the waning moon

4. The 15th day of the waning moon or 14th day of waning moon in months with 30-days (the new moon).

On these days, Buddhists attend the ceremonies at the temple. Early in the morning, they prepare food, soft drink, desert, fruits, flowers, etc. and then take them to the temple. At the end of the ceremony, Buddhists pray for all the good things they have done and that they wish to go to their relatives who have passed away. In addition, they also wish that this good karma will radiate and go to all the people and animals that they have dealt with, and to ask for forgiveness for anything untoward they have done to them (intentionally or otherwise).

In the next section we will look at the Buddhist festivals.

Buddhist Festivals

The principal Buddhist festivals are Buddhist Lent Day (the start), the End of the Buddhist Lent Day, and Devorohana (or Tak-Bat-Devo).

Buddhist Lent Day

Buddhist Lent, or *Khao Phansa*, begins on the first waning day of the 8th lunar month, and lasts for three months to the 15th waxing day of the 11th lunar month. This period is during the rainy season and is when the monks temporarily stop the practice of travelling to other places to teach and give sermons; instead retreating to their monasteries.

This has been the practice since Buddha's time. Though their movement is itself restricted, no actual restriction is placed on their duty of spreading the Buddha's message. As such, people travel to the temples to listen to monks deliver sermons and to receive teachings within the confines of the monasteries.

This practice was started by Buddha as a way to address the concerns of the farmers who complained that wandering monks during the rainy season caused damage to their crops. As a result, Buddha imposed restrictions on the movement of the monks during the rainy season.

At this time, the young monks get a chance to train under the guidance of senior monks which can be an enriching experience for both parties.

This is also the period when the monks get ample time to meditate and to contemplate. This period is sort of a camping period as they have plenty of time to study the scriptures, to practice meditation, and can improve their morality, concentration and wisdom.

Furthermore, due to the presence and company of the senior monks, this is also a preferred and beneficial time for Buddhist believers to be ordained into the order. Additionally, and for that very same reason, large number of novices and families of the monks also congregate in the monasteries to benefit from the sermons and discourses delivered during that period. The novices get to pledge to follow the right path and to abstain from doing incorrect things such as smoking and consuming alcohol, and lots of positive energy is created from these gatherings.

End of the Buddhist Lent Day

The 15th day of the waxing moon of the 11th lunar month marks the end of Buddhist Lent (or *Auk Phansa*). This also marks the end of the rainy season and the monk's retreat period; this ending their restriction of movement. The End of Buddhist Lent Day is also one of the holy days for both monks and novices, and is the time the

monks approach one another to atone for any mistake or offense caused or committed by them.

Buddhist believers (or novices) celebrate by gathering at the temples, offering food to the monks, praying, meditating, listening to Dharma and observing moral disciplines. It is a joyful day and in addition to the above, an alms giving ceremony known as Tak-Bat-Devo is organized on the following day to celebrate.

Devorohana (Tak-Bat-Devo)

Legend says that after Buddha attained enlightenment, he travelled extensively in India to deliver sermons and spread his message of Dharma. During these travels, he even enlightened and initiated his father, King Shoddodhana; his step-mother, Mahaprajapati; his wife, Yashodhara; his son, Rahula; and many others into the Buddhist tradition. It was then that he remembered his own mother, Queen Mahamaya, who passed away seven days after his birth. Lord Buddha wanted to repay her for her love and kindness so, seven years after attaining enlightenment, the Buddha went to the heaven where his mother was residing, stayed with her for three months, and taught her 'the profound truth' (*Abhidhamma Pitaka*). As the end of the three month retreat was approaching, the Buddha then came down from heaven and the people were overjoyed. They celebrated his coming back to the earth by offering food, practicing moral discipline and participating in the discourses and meditation.

This event came to be called Tak-Bat-Devo or Devorohana and, as mentioned, is usually celebrated the day after the last day of the Buddhist Lent.

Buddhist Ceremony

Offering Food to the Monks

Offering food is one of the oldest rituals of Buddhism and is considered a meritorious act because it teaches people not to be selfish, to share with others, and to promote generosity, kindness and compassion.

This ceremony has been practiced since the time of the Buddha, and monks and nuns leave their monastery very early in the morning carrying their alms bowl. They walk barefoot and silently in single file with the oldest or the senior most monk leading the group.

Those people willing to give alms stand in a line waiting for the monks to pass. Often, as a mark of respect, the laypeople kneel and some even remove their footwear as they place their offerings in the bowls. The ceremony takes place in a simple manner without even exchange of wishes and pleasantries. Sometimes, the senior monk in the group might wish to use this opportunity to deliver a brief sermon.

The practice of giving alms is not considered an act of charity but as an act aimed at developing a spiritual connection between householders and monks. While the householders take up the responsibility of providing for the basic, physical needs of the monks, the monks in turn look to fulfilling the higher, spiritual needs of the laypeople.

The offering of food to the monks can be done even in the temple or at home where people who are interested in offering food to the monks either bring food to the temple or invite the monks to their house.

When offering food to the monks in the Buddhist festival, *Tak-Bat-Devo*, the laypeople first sit in the temple for a sermon to be delivered. After the sermon the monks leave the main chapel where all the people would be waiting with their offerings. The monks, holding their bowls, walk in a straight line and people place their offerings in those bowls. When the bowl gets full, it is emptied into another plate by a layman so that the monk can continue taking alms. As always, women should take care not to touch the monks while placing food in the bowl.

After the monks have delivered a series of sermons and finished eating, all the food is placed on the table, and everybody there can partake of the food.

Become an Ordained Monk

The rules and procedures to be followed while carrying out an ordination ceremony are contained in the *Buddhist Monastic Rule* of the sangha.

The ceremony has not changed since the time of the Buddha and is carried out in Pali, the language of Buddhism at the time of origin, and which glorifies and establishes the importance of the ceremony. However, since Buddhism has permeated to various countries and cultures with different languages, the phrases in Pali are also translated into local languages for the convenience and understanding of family, friends, and well-wishers of the monks who have come to witness the ordaining ceremony.

To become a monk:

- One must be over 20 years of age and should have the consent of his parents.

- He should not have committed a crime such as murder, rape especially of a nun, causing injury to the Buddha, causing a rift in the sangha, pretend to be a monk without ordination, leaving the sangha to join another religion.

- Should not be a eunuch.

A person with an infectious disease, a fugitive, a debtor and one with physical disabilities cannot be ordained as they will be unable to stand the rigors of monastic life. But, if they have already been ordained, then their ordination will stand valid and cannot be dismissed on the above grounds.

For the ordination ceremony to take place, twelve monks from the sangha are required, one of whom should have been a monk for at least 10 years. This senior monk would later take charge as the preceptor of the would-be monk and take care of him during his monastic life while the young believer is expected to take care of the preceptor, just as he would take care of his father.

The ceremony begins with the parents of the young believer presenting him his monk robes and his bowl. At this stage, the young man is expected to ask his parents for forgiveness for any mistakes committed on his part in any form. With the parents' blessings, the would-be monk approaches the Sangha.

The person is then briefly instructed about the ceremony before being given his new name (this is to keep him reminded of his new life and the new purpose and responsibilities that come with it).

He is then sent to stand away from the main group of monks, following which two monks will go and test him on his suitability to be a monk. After examining him, the two monks return to the

other monks and let them know about the test. The candidate is now called back and asked the same questions. They give their answers in front of all the monks.

Since one cannot be forced into monkhood, the young man is supposed to make a formal request to the Sangha to be ordained as a monk. All monks participating in the ordination should sit within arm's length of each other, and the two monks of the sangha make an announcement that the person has made a formal request for ordination and that he has been found suitable to be made a monk. They continue to propose this two more times. This is the time when any objection (if any) to the ordination of the person can be raised and any objection leads to the denial of monkhood for the person. In the event of no objection, the person is declared a monk.

The preceptor of the newly ordained monk will then instruct him on the four disrobing offences which are to be treated as the four dangers to monkhood and which are to be avoided: sexual intercourse, murder, false claims of attainment, and stealing. He will also receive instructions on the four basic needs of a monk: food gathered as alms, robes made of rags, a shelter under a tree, and medicines made from urine. With these instructions the ceremony comes to a close.

This is a very important practice. Live your daily life in a way that you never lose yourself. When you are carried away with your worries, fears, cravings, anger, and desire, you run away from yourself and you lose yourself. The practice is always to go back to oneself.

Thich Nhat Hanh

Chapter 4. Mind and Wisdom Exercises

Wise Reflection

Wise reflection or *Yoniso Manasikara* means using the mind skilfully.

Using the mind skilfully is to understand and gain an insight into what the consequences of our thoughts and actions would be like, to understand the true nature of things, and to accept the hard truths of life.

The literal meaning of Yoniso is 'the place of origin from where everything starts and from where everything begins', but the true meaning says that Yoniso means 'to get to the core of something in order to perfect your understanding with regard to the consequences'. Manasikara means to direct, or lead, the attention to the core (heart, depth).

It must be understood that plain concentration is not enough to gain wisdom. To gain wisdom requires the ability to pay wise attention to accomplish things. Buddha was deeply interested in the subject of wise reflection and said the following about it

> *"I say that the getting rid of anxieties and*
> *troubles is possible for one who knows and*
> *sees, not for one who does not know and see."*

According to Buddha, a person who knows and sees is the one who reflects wisely, and the person who does not know and see is the one who reflects unwisely.

For example, a person who reflects unwisely will start to see anxieties and troubles that have not yet arisen; whereas, a person who reflects unwisely and who is already facing anxieties and troubles will see their effects increase. In contrast, a person who reflects wisely will either never see these troubles or anxieties, or will be able to avoid them when they do appear—wise reflection can, and will, make them disappear.

From his enlightenment until his death, the Buddha kept emphasizing that mental suffering is caused by wrong thinking; and this is where Yoniso Manasikara comes to the rescue: wise reflection helps one to develop and nurture the wisdom and intelligence to consider things using critical and analytical reflection, as well as systematic and reasoned attention with a view to developing right thinking.

Insight Meditation

Insight meditation, or Vipassana, is the process of knowing and gaining proper understanding about oneself.

When we experience suffering, we usually blame our external world; this could be God, it could be people, or it could be circumstances. However, Buddha identified this is incorrect. In reality, our suffering is actually caused by our own internal, not external, world: it is our own thoughts, feelings, and emotions that cause pain and suffering to us.

Consequently, changing our external world or trying to manipulate our external world is no guarantee of happiness. What can give us everlasting happiness is a mind which is pure and free of unhealthy thoughts, and one that is free from desire and ignorance (the root causes of suffering). This purification is possible with Vipassana meditation.

Vipassana is a technique that ensures success only if we are willing to devote our efforts to our internal world, instead of placing all this responsibility on our external world.

Meditation techniques can be classified into two types: insight meditation (Vipassana), and tranquillity meditation (concentration).

In tranquillity meditation (concentration), we practice by trying to focus our mind on one object until we develop enough concentration, attain stillness, calmness, and are able to filter out all mental afflictions, such as anger, stress, jealousy, hatred, impatience, etc. The only problem here is that when one stops meditating, the mental afflictions can come straight back and reside where they were before—in our minds. Insight meditation, or Vipassana is different.

Vipassana does not stop at developing plain concentration, it also develops wisdom. Vipassana is about developing mindfulness. You see, in mindfulness, we do not fix out attention on one thing, we just let things, ideas, thoughts, emotions, feelings, etc., come and pass but without our reacting to them. Vipassana is about realizing and making note of each feeling, sensation, and emotion but without responding to it. Eventually, these unhealthy mental factors vacate our minds leaving it pure.

Vipassana deals with dissecting the mind to separate reality from delusion, and is a powerful and intense form of dissecting the mind to examine its components. It's almost confronting the truth and reality with a view to gaining freedom from suffering and, ultimately, enlightenment.

Bibliography

Buddhist Beliefs. (n.d.). Retrieved June 27, 2015, from Religion Facts: http://www.religionfacts.com/buddhism/beliefs

Hagen, S. (2013). *Buddhism Plain and Simple*. Singapore: Tuttle.

Hanh, T. N. (1999). *The Heart of the Buddha's Teaching: Transforming Suffering into Peace, Joy, and Liberation*. New York: Broadway Books.

History of Buddhism. (n.d.). Retrieved June 26, 2015, from About Buddhism: http://www.aboutbuddhism.org/history-of-buddhism.htm/

Lama, D. (2006). *The Universe in a Single Atom: The Convergence of Science and Spirituality*. New York: Harmony.

Lama, D. (2013). *What Matters Most: Conversations on Anger, Compassion, and Action*. Charlottesville: Hampton Roads Publishing.

Sayagaw, M. (2009, March 16). *What is Threefold Training* . Retrieved June 28, 2015, from Yellow Robe: http://www.yellowrobe.com/practice/the-threefold-training/221-what-is-threefold-training.html

Thuan, X. (N.D.). *Science and Buddhism*. Retrieved June 25, 2015, from Universitie Interdisciplinaire De Paris: http://uip.edu/en/articles-en/science-and-buddhism

Verhoeven, M. (2013, Summer). Science through Buddhist Eyes. *The New Atlantis, 39*, 107-118. Retrieved from The new Atlantis.

II

A Beginner's Guide to Meditation

"Our prime purpose in this life is to help others. And if you can't help them, at least don't hurt them."

His Holiness, the XIV Dalai Lama

Preface

I first started to practice meditation when I was 7 years old. My family are Buddhists and I always went with my grandmother to the temple. Every Buddhist holy day, my grandmother would go there early in the morning, take the required 8 precepts, and practice meditation. She would stay at the temple overnight and, when she departed the following morning, would leave the 8 precepts behind, take the 5 precepts for normal life, and then go home. She did this 4 times a month, on holy days, for her entire life.

My own first experience of meditating was when the temple hosted a ten day meditation camp for monks, nuns, and Buddhists. Just a little girl, I took the 8 precepts and then was expected to perform the same as the adults: we woke up at 3:30 in the morning and I washed myself. At 4 a.m., we were ready for the day and all chanted for an hour. We then meditated from 5 to 6. Following which we had breakfast—the first of the day's two meals. We were then permitted 2 hours to relax, and then we practiced meditation until lunch at 11. The practice started again from 1 to 4 p.m., followed by washing and having soft drinks (in place of dinner). At 6 p.m., we all chanted again for an hour, before the final hour of meditation. We all then went to sleep at 9 p.m.

At the time, even though I didn't understand that much about the purpose of meditating, I knew I enjoyed it. Later, I discovered what meditation gives you, and I've since been looking for how to improve my ability, how to reach the goal of meditation, as well as how to achieve it without hurting my body. This book is useful for anyone who wants to start practicing meditation in a correct manner, and has been written from my own meditation experiences.

My book, A Beginner's Guide to Meditation, will help you in getting started with meditation both successfully and in a short time. You will then see how meditation can and will improve your life in many ways. Of course, to do this you must try it yourself to appreciate what I write about, to see what I mean, to sense what I feel, and to achieve what I have—the true happiness

Duangta Wanthong Mondi, August 2015

Table of Contents

Table of Figures

Figure 1 - The Author Meditating

Chapter 1. Getting Ready for Meditation

Preparing for Meditation

There are few things that you have to consider before starting your meditation exercise, but these are essential towards the success of your exercise practice; so it's a good idea to ensure that these are correct.

- Clothing

    Comfortable and appropriate clothing can make all the difference when planning for meditation. You want to be wearing something which is both loose and allows you to easily relax in. Perhaps you've seen pictures of people meditating before, and noticed that many of them wearing a plain, light, and loose cotton outfit—this is selected for a reason: it's complete, it's comfortable, and it helps you settle nicely into the mood. Conversely, if your shirt is too tight, or your pants are too rough on your skin, then they're going to quickly distract you, and prevent you from achieving what you set out to do. Your clothes are the first step towards framing your mind for meditation, moving towards the desired focus, and gaining the level of energy required. Indeed, obtaining the right clothing will make peace and contentment much easier to attain.

Figure 2 - Wear Comfortable Clothing

- Breathing

    It might sound a little strange, but breathing is the next step in preparing for your meditation. Slow, regular breathing is the key to settling your mind and starting your meditation, so try and establish a breathing pattern as soon as you can. If you can do this before you begin meditation, you may find the practice much easier. For beginners, the basic breathing technique refers to simple inhales and exhales, such as when you're sitting relaxed or even asleep.

When you breathe, try to remain still and feel the sensations of your breathing in your chest and abdomen, as they swell and rise on the inward breath, and collapse and fall on the outward breath. While practicing your breathing, try your best to eliminate all the thoughts in your mind, as this is both the key to effective meditation and, with all the distractions, noises around you, one of the most challenging. So, as you focus only on your breathing, as you first inhale you sense mentally the air passing in through your nose; then, as you exhale gently through slightly parted lips, you feel this slow expulsion of air in your mind also. Next, repeat the process again and again until your body naturally conforms to the process.

When you're ready to dig deeper into your relaxation, make a conscious switch with your breathing by taking slow, deep breaths, counting slowly to 3 as you inhale...1, 2, 3 and then letting the air slowly out to the same count as you exhale... 1, 2, 3. As you improve, you may find you can increase the inhale/exhale rate, to 5, 7, etc. Repeat this slow breathing process to boost the supply of oxygen that is needed to further relax your thoughts. Thankfully, you can practice your breathing anywhere and anytime it suits you.

- Place and Time

There is no recommended time or place for meditation because it all depends on the individual and their choices. Generally, the best place to perform your daily meditation would be a pleasant, quiet, and comfortable area free from disturbances and distractions. However, before you think of meditating in bed, doing the practice in there is not advisable as there's a high risk of falling into sleep after a few minutes or so. When you do find a suitable place, you should try and ensure that you can use the same place at the same time every day (as stressing out looking for your next meditation venue isn't great for a focused mind).

Though the ideal time for meditation is between 3 and 4 a.m., this is not practical for many folk due to scheduling conflicts and a myriad of other reasons. So, the next best time is either early morning or late at night; but again, it depends on your time, availability, and preference; and is something that you should identify as the best time for your own meditation.

Sitting Meditation

Because its primary purpose is to relax your thoughts and lessen the amount of unnecessary mind activity required to achieve a certain level of consciousness, sitting meditation doesn't require any complicated techniques: you practice sitting meditation with your eyes closed.

Figure 3 - Hands in Lap, Thumbs Touching, Feet Flat

Figure 4 - Hands in Lap, Thumbs Touching, Foot on Thigh

Figure 5 - Hands on Knee Thumbs Touching, Feet Flat

Figure 6 - Hands on Knee Thumbs Touching, Foot on Thigh

Ideally, it is done by sitting on the ground, on a meditation mat, or cushion to alleviate any strain on your body. However, not everyone is comfortable in this position, so meditating while sitting on a chair is acceptable as long as the body isn't leaning back and being supported.

- Posture

  Sit up straight and don't lean back. It is important to make sure that you alone are supporting your upper body. Tilt your pelvis forward slightly to push your butt backwards and your abdomen forwards. This posture will automatically and naturally arch your lower back, and help your body to relax.

- Legs

  There are two different options for positioning your legs:

  o Sitting in a crossed-leg position with one foot on top of the opposite thigh, while the other one rests underneath the opposing leg (refer to Figure 3).

  o Sitting in a crossed-leg position with your foot resting on top of your thighs (refer to Figure 4).

- Hands

  There are also two different options for the positions of your hands:

  o Hold your hands in front of you and with the tips of the fingers and thumb of your left hand, against those of the right to form an oval. This process will help maintain and circulate the same level of energy through your body (refer to Figure 3 and Figure 4).

o   Place your right hand flat in the palm of your left hand and then place your thumb tips together (refer to Figure 5 and Figure 6).

Walking Meditation

Although many people associate meditation with a sitting position, walking meditation is actually a lot easier for some because they can both feel the intense energy of their own movements while also achieving the required level of consciousness. To compare, with the walking method you can focus and meditate as you use your muscles; whereas with the sitting method there is a high risk of falling asleep or getting distracted by different thoughts and anxieties running through your mind.

Naturally, meditation while walking has different requirements: for safety's sake, your eyes must be open while performing this practice; and you should try and feel your body's movements as part of the art of concentration.

In walking meditation, you do not divert your thoughts or attention outside of the real world because you need to be alert and consider the elements and environment around you while practicing. For instance, though you do have to concentrate on your inner energy, you must also ensure you don't trip or fall down a hole.

- Posture

  Stand up straight and, to help prepare your body to obtain focus, ensure your neck and back are straight. Slouching may bring on negative effects, such as making it difficult to find your level of consciousness.

- Legs

  Stand on flat feet and bend your knees a little to help your blood circulation, and energy flow throughout your body.

Figure 7 - Walking Meditation Posture

- Chest

  Drop your shoulders and cave your chest slightly to release all tension from your upper body. This way, it's easier to calm your breathing, and to maintain a steady supply of oxygen while you walk.

- Hands

  For most practitioners, you maintain and circulate your level of energy by placing the tips of the thumb and forefinger together on each hand. However, if preferred, another position is where you can place your hands down by your side while walking. Furthermore, others have also suggested that placing your hands behind your lower back, with the right hand holding the wrist of the left hand, is also a good position (**Note**: this is the author's preferred hand position for walking meditation).

Figure 8 - The Author and Her Preferred Hand Position for Standing Meditation

Knowing Your Mind

Our mind is the initiator of the things that we experience in our lives. As such, every one of us should take positive steps to understand the nature of our own mind; and, regardless of whether our mind is filled with good or bad thoughts, be aware that our thoughts are powerful enough to take control of any situation. There needs to be an element of caution here, as if you are not strong or cautious enough, it can lead you to a worsening condition.

We will now look at our mind's make-up.

Ordinary Mind vs. Innermost Essence

The nature of our mind is divided into 2 parts: the ordinary mind and the inner mind. The ordinary mind (*Sem*), is the promoter of negative thoughts in our lives, those stimulators of hatred and ill feelings, and the agent that loses hope and causes weariness. An ordinary mind sees the situation as it is in the outside world—hopeless and irrevocable; and looks for the destruction of great ideas and conscience. Furthermore, Sem is also the nature of the mind that conceals the existence of the innermost essence of the second part of the human mind—the inner mind.

The inner mind (*Rigpa*) contains both wisdom and awareness and allows our subconscious to understand and appreciate everything. With Rigpa, we can look at all the positive perspectives of life in the midst of all the worries, undesirable events and attitudes that are present; and, not only will we be aware of them, but we can also address them in a calm and rational manner. Unfortunately, Sem is able to obscure this particular state of awareness, thereby increasing anxiety and other negative thoughts and emotions, which hinder our path to achieving our goals.

It is clear to see that Rigpa is the mental state that we are trying to open up and develop when we meditate: in doing so, we look forward to achieving positive thought which, when perfected, will overcome and conquer all hindrances.

Take a few moments to evaluate your own mind now, and to determine which of these natures of mind is most prominent now. It may be a bit confusing to actually take control of your mind when you believe it to be in an ordinary state; however, healthy, stress free thoughts are choices which we should all consider as being more powerful and more welcome than those filled with uncertainties, doubts, and fears.

In Buddhism, everything is circular—there is cause and there is effect; and, the mind is no different—our internal thoughts and feelings affect our lives. As we well know, our 'inner life' is influenced by events around us, which in turn affects our reaction to these events—our behavior. This reaction again changes what is going on around us, and affects our inner life again—it is a circular process. The mind is also said to affect our karma. Karma is how our deliberate actions lead to future consequences in our lives—again, cause and effect. Moreover, our deliberate thoughts and our inner life can also affect this: negative inner thoughts can create negative energy in much the same way as negative actions.

We only have to look at babies to know that our minds are essentially pure, and negative or distracting thoughts like hate and worry enter into our mind from outside—they are not things we are born with. However, it is encouraging to know that this negativity can be removed through meditation and attention to our spirituality: meditation purifies the mind, liberating it from earthly things that muddle and confuse it, allowing the meditator to feel both cleansed and free.

In Tibetan Buddhism, the mind has three inseparable elements: perceptions, projections, and phenomena. The mind perceives things around us through the use of our senses: nothing around us exists without us perceiving it. We then project our own thoughts onto these items, and assign them labels so our brains can readily organize them. Once labelled, concepts such as our sense of self become phenomena that we then project onto our perceptions—once again, it is circular. Essentially, humans are nothing more than a product of our own physical and psychological processes.

Enlightenment occurs when one can observe their own perceptions and know that they are of the mind, and they are insubstantial. The enlightened individual observes these phenomena and lets them go. Consequently, earthly emotions like anger, excitement, and fear have no effect, because an enlightened person sees them for what they are—perceptions. They are also able to see their dreams in the same way, and to change them as required. As I hope you can see, when one has this flexibility of mind it enhances their ability to control emotions, desires, etc.

Buddhism also emphasizes that there are different levels and categories of the mind, including: a waking state, a dreaming state, and a state of enlightenment. However, there are also many more subconscious levels of the mind that are imperceptible to us. In addition, there is also the concept of the primary mind, which processes things as a whole; and the secondary mind, which processes the details. As we can see, the mind itself is a layered and multifaceted entity, and by being aware of its complexities, meditation can help us access those deeper layers and help us to control our thoughts in an extremely beneficial manner.

Another important step to understanding the nature of the mind is to understand the three marks of existence: inadequacy, impermanence, and existence/not-self. The first mark is inadequacy: one of the major goals of a traditional Buddhist is to eradicate their sense of incompetence and insufficiency, and dispel negative emotions, such as frustration and sadness, as well as physical sensations, such as pain. The second mark is impermanence: the awareness that we are just a temporary entity and are just passing through this life on this Earth—we will die. The final mark of existence is the idea of our actual existence/our 'not-self': this can be difficult to grasp for many people new to Buddhism or meditation, but the basis of this concept is that our consciousness and sensations are not ourselves; and therefore, our true selves transcend these.

Of course, there are many more complex details to the Buddhist interpretation of the mind, but these are the ones most related to meditation; and, understanding these ideas can be extremely beneficial to those starting to practice meditation.

Bring Your Mind to the Present

One of the most important aspects of meditation in the modern world is bringing your mind to the present moment—the here and now. It is both extremely tempting and easy to dwell on things that have happened in the past, or to focus so much on your goals and worries for the future, that you actually miss what is happening in the present.

Bringing your mind to the present is mainly an exercise in concentration and focus, and is why meditation is such an extremely effective way of helping with this. Meditating will empty your mind of all concerns that are not relevant to the now, the present moment. So, from this point onwards, try to apply the principle of observing events around you and letting them go from your life. If something negative or stressful is happening, just ignore it: don't start to worry about all the horrible things that could come out of it as this just generates negative energy and pulls you out of the present moment. Instead, take a few deep breaths, and continue to focus on the present to improve the situation.

It is also extremely important to focus on the positive sides of your present situation as much as possible, no matter how small they are. Take a few minutes each day to enjoy something that makes you happy: maybe it's reading a chapter of your favorite book, or taking a walk in your favorite park. While you are there, stay in the moment and enjoy these things, it will boost your positive energy and make you more active and cheerful. Another thing that is important is to assess all you are thankful for whenever you start to feel pessimistic, angry, or sad about something. Even if they are small things, this is a great reminder that there is good in the world—in your world—and that you are lucky to be a part of it.

Something else that is very difficult to do when it comes to staying in the present is to successfully work towards your goals. You are probably wondering how to make any sort of progress if you avoid thinking about the future. The answer here is to set a series of steps towards your goal, and then immerse yourself in the first step. Don't try and think about the next step, or the previous step if you're further from your goal, just focus on the current one. Try to detach yourself from your end result, because though important, it can be detrimental to your current work if you're focused on it too much. Allocating all of your focus to your daily activities is much more productive.

This level of focus can also even improve your intelligence. You see, when we aren't living in the present moment, it is hard for us to access the full extent of our knowledge and the things that we have learned. But when we clear our minds, truly live in the present, and focus on the task at hand, it is incredible what our brains can do. Therefore, not only can meditation improve performance, but studies have shown that it improves cognition, memory, and even test-taking ability.

Key to remaining present is to work on minimizing the number of self-related distracting thoughts you process throughout your day. Often, when we are struggling with something, we are actually our own worst enemy. When we are faltering it's often because our thoughts are turned inwards ('in our own heads'), instead of thinking about the current problem. For example, instead of concentrating on what your peers are saying during a work meeting, you're thinking about your own problems: about the argument you had at home last night, or all the emails that are mounting up. Focus here is crucial, both during meditation practice and throughout the day; and, you will discover that incorporating the Buddhist principle of 'no-self' into your own life is very beneficial.

Banish Negativity and Be Happy

One of the biggest ways meditation can affect your life is to rid it of negative energy. By ridding yourself of this negativity, you will immediately feel more positive (cause and effect). This might sound like a bit of a con, but it isn't: quite simply, if you remove a weight from something, the load is less. A common goal is to find true happiness amidst who you are, and meditation is a great way to do this. That is also why meditation is often recommended as a way to cope with mental health issues such as depression and anxiety. While general breath-based meditation will naturally improve your mood over time, meditation performed with specific focus on positivity will make an incredible difference to your well-being.

Whenever you meditate, take time to think about the positive elements in your life and really notice them for what they are. It is often difficult for us to notice positive things when we are stressed, because they are so easy to take for granted. So, notice the positive things around you, and in your life; and think about how you are going to carry them with you throughout your day so they are there when you need them. If you subsequently find yourself in a situation where you start to get stressed, think of one of your positives. Over time, you will then associate this positivity with calm, and you'll be able to handle stressful situations much better and with a more optimistic outlook.

Another great benefit to becoming more positive is that it will attract other positive individuals. Maintaining a positive environment is a sure-fire and great way to stay happy; and, if you are a force of positivity, it may also help others around you who may be struggling with their own stress or emotions.

Of course, staying positive is much easier said than done, but it is important to keep working at it, even when it does get difficult. Try to make meditation and positive thinking a habit as soon as you can. Even if you are having a hard time staying positive, or you forget to meditate one day, just start again tomorrow and keep trying. Eventually, it will become much easier. Also, take notice of yourself, and if you find yourself slipping into a rut of negativity, analyze what's happening to see if you can try to break that cycle. When you're fixated on something negative, it is easy to start noticing all the other negative things in your life (no matter how small), which will only lead to further frustration and stress—focusing on staying calm is crucial.

Meditation can also be used to improve many different elements of your life: from physical healing to job performance, and from increased focus to greater productivity, there are so many benefits to daily meditation practice. With a little focus and dedication, anyone can make meditation a part of their routine and reap a multitude of benefits.

Benefits of Meditation

As we've already covered, there are both physical and mental benefits to be found through meditation, including mind control, inner peace, and great wisdom. In fact, each individual will have different reasons for engaging in this practice, but what is important is that you start practicing as soon as you can because these positive effects are only attainable if done regularly.

Mind Control

Though these two words are often associated with telekinesis or some other supernatural power, mind control in meditation refers to your ability to manage all the distractions around you. Our world is filled with negative thoughts and realities, such as sadness, depression, anxiety, fear and doubt; and meditation helps to develop your mind towards the highest level of control. In fact, when you become proficient enough, you can transform all your negative energy into positive energy with your mind.

Inner Peace

Peace or tranquillity is a state of mind where a person is totally free from any form of anxiety. Having already read this far, you can see now how this can be achieved by meditation; and, as inner peace comes from within you and your senses—a supreme contentment that is just there, deep inside of you—the kind of harmony you will receive here is different from that offered by the material world.

Great Wisdom

As you may know, knowledge and wisdom are entirely different. Knowledge is a skill which can be developed and achieved by studying hard, but it often takes years of practice, enormous mental effort, as well as a desire and willingness to learn. In contrast, wisdom is more of a special gift of intuition and fair judgement that is present in different forms, i.e. sensitive instincts, hereditary factors, mental capability and breeding.

Meditation offers wisdom to an advanced level of thinking, and can make situations far clearer and easier to understand. It makes learning and comprehending many wonders of life much simpler, even if the clues themselves are difficult to explain.

Uses of Meditation in Your Life

Mind relaxation also brings two important advantages to our everyday lives, which should never be taken for granted: healing and performance enhancement.

Healing

One of the biggest benefits of meditation is in its healing powers. Opening the mind by meditation, and the stability this offers, is ideal for allowing the body to repair itself. Meditation can help us both physically and mentally: physically, by allowing our minds to recover from the exhaustions of daily life, and mentally by either improving the symptoms of an existing mental condition, or by decreasing the chances of one ever occurring.

Meditation has a number of mental and emotional advantages, and there is scientific basis that also shows there are a number of medical advantages and remedies to different types of body illnesses.

A Harvard Medical School research comparing those who performed meditation practices for a significant period of time versus those who didn't, showed that those who did practice developed a "disease fighting gene".

According to author Jay Winner, stress is the major cause of a variety of illnesses. In fact, people who suffer with negativity and stress often develop health issues, ranging from simple to serious. Some examples of afflictions caused by stress are constipation, headache, ulcers, muscle and joint problems, high blood pressure, cancers, etc.

If you feel stressed, you know you need to relax—relaxation opposes stress. Therefore, if your mind is relaxed and at peace, the systems in your body are functioning normally and correctly, and will both prevent and fight the toxins inside of you. Moreover, scientific studies have confirmed the positive benefits of meditation. John L. Craven, found that meditation consistently reduced symptoms of stress-related conditions. This applied mainly to anxiety, but also to a number of other conditions, including chronic pain, hypertension, and asthma.

Meditation is also helpful for easing symptoms of chronic physical illnesses or problems. Our body's resistance to disease and pain drops when we are stressed and, due to our brain's 'fight or flight' response, this creates adrenaline. When this occurs, the body's repairing mechanisms—the ones that generate new cells and create antibodies to fight off infection—cannot work efficiently, thereby increasing the risk of sickness.

Additionally, meditation benefits many conditions unrelated to stress. Studies by Harvard professor, Herbert Benson, indicates that meditation can improve symptoms of serious diseases, such as cancer and AIDS, as well as assist with coughing, nausea, general tension, and pain throughout the entire body. The relaxed state of meditation allows the body to release tension stored throughout our busy workdays, and offers much needed pain relief. Likewise, it can also help reduce our respiratory system and our heart rate, as well as reducing stress-based cortisol in the brain.

Furthermore, the deep breathing associated with meditation is especially helpful, because the oxygen you are receiving is a life support for your body functions, and the relaxing rhythm of this deep breathing will further decrease the amount of tension that you feel.

Earlier, we mentioned the healing benefits of meditation for troubled mental or emotional states. Nowadays, with ever busier and hectic lives, it's almost as if we are in constant worry about our everyday problems; and, it is therefore important that we create a positive state of mind to help manage this—meditation can help us achieve this state.

Meditation can assist us in viewing our problems in a different light; and, by observing them calmly, instead of feeling stressed and irritable, you will be able to manage them and let them go. Moreover, by helping to release the negative energy, thoughts, and tension that the person has been carrying around with them, meditation can also help struggles with emotional trauma or past stressful events, allowing the person to move forward with positivity and calm.

The spiritual element of meditation can also be extremely helpful for many people. You see, when the focus is on spirituality, meditation can engender a feeling of a sense of connection with something greater than themselves. This can create a much more positive outlook in the meditator, reduce stress, and make them happier. It also helps the meditator to feel closer to, and connected with, the natural world. This itself can help improve strength, reduce muscle tension, and reduce instances of the 'placebo effect' (where, by expecting to have a certain symptom, a person then creates that symptom).

To summarize, the healing powers of meditation are actually quite formidable and can benefit sufferers of many different conditions.

Enhancing your performance

Meditation can also be used to enhance performance in many aspects of our lives: at work, in physical areas, such as athletics, and even with our social lives. Indeed, dedicated focus for just a few minutes a day can drastically improve the quality of life for many people.

If you are stressed, your mental and physiological ability suffer. That is why there's a great chance that you'll perform poorly in the office or at home. Being stressed means your ability to think clearly and your response to certain situations can become dull and incoherent.

As a result, many successful professionals use regular meditation to keep them composed and focused throughout what would otherwise be stressful lives. This composure, in turn, helps increase their professional successes. For example, meditating before going to work each morning will help you stay present during the workday, which could lead you to increased idea generation and better decision making. It can also increase your enjoyment of your work because, by focus on the positives, the stress and negative aspects of the job that were present before no longer weigh you down. The knock-on effect of this is your personal environment changes and others will become attracted to you and want to work with you. It may also make it easier to take professional risks without the normally associated extra anxiety that comes with it.

Again, we touched on this before, one of the most important points when meditating to improve job success is to stay focused on the present and remain in the moment (this applies to any area though, not just performance enhancement). While it is great to have goals and to know what you want out of your career, it is much easier to achieve those goals if you are successful in the present moment and invest yourself in the projects you are currently working on. Also, if you ever find yourself in a stressful situation at work, it will help to meditate. Take a few minutes in your office to just close your eyes and focus on your breathing. This will keep you from being overwhelmed by the situation and allow you to remain calm.

Naturally, meditation is also a great tool for athletes looking to improve their performance. While working physically towards your athletic goals is obviously very important, it is hard to make progress without a strong, clear and determined mind. However, a few minutes of quiet meditation that allows you to clear your mind and focus on your breath will not only release tension that may be negatively affecting your performance, but can also empty your mind of any self-doubt that may stand in the way. Take time to notice the things that are happening around you and then let them go. Once you have done that you can use visualization—where you picture yourself achieving your athletic goals easily and with perfect form—as many times and as often as you want.

Indeed, positive visualization has been proven to improve athletic performance. Studies in Psychology Today and The Journal of Sport & Exercise Psychology have shown that visualization activates the neurons that control the muscles that perform the exercise without physically doing it: the brain is essentially training without exerting any physical effort—this is a technique used by many Olympic athletes.

As meditation increases activity in the cortex of the brain, this helps us process emotions more efficiently and makes us feel happier. By doing so, it also decreases the feelings of fear and stress that are associated with socializing, and can thereby improve our social lives. This is especially beneficial to those struggling with communal anxiety, as removing these negative feelings makes us more willing to participate in the community. As you probably know, feeling happier can affect your social life in many positive ways, especially in attracting others closer to you.

If you practice regularly, meditation also offers improvements to your mental and emotional stability, including enhancing creativity and focus, increasing peace-of-mind, decreasing worries and anxiety, and removing uncertainties. As can be seen, meditation can bring many advantages to your performance enhancement, not least of which is equipping you with the necessary tools to manage and conquer any given situation confidently and calmly.

Chapter 2. Basic Knowledge about Meditation

In this chapter, we will first look at the basic knowledge of meditation; and second, we will distinguish between the terms concentration and meditation.

Concentration

Focusing your mind on a particular subject involves a process called Concentration (*Samadhi*). The word concentrate refers to an exclusive mental application where your mind is focused on a particular subject or object to then develop your thoughts. Concentration requires both will and energy to attain the required level; and, as this can be demanding, often leads to exhaustion if done incorrectly. Mental involvement is often one of the major factors required to attain any goal; and, though concentration means focusing internally, it must still keep you aware of your outside world. This enables you to think clearly about a subject, enables you to become involved with that topic, and may even enable you to solve or manage it. The purpose of being in this state of mind is to be able to gain control over something by using your mind's energy, while simultaneously ignoring everything else that may distract you.

Levels of Concentration

While practicing concentration, you will experience different thoughts and feelings in your mind, depending on how much focus there currently is in your mind: there are three levels of concentration, called The Threefold Concentration, and these are: momentary concentration, access concentration, and absorption concentration.

Momentary Concentration

Momentary concentration (*Kanika Samadhi*), is the preliminary stage towards achieving the supreme stage, or completely fixed concentration. At this stage, your level of focus is already determined, but your thoughts will likely jump about from one subject to another without any break in your mind's energy. This doesn't mean that your concentration is inconsistent or weak, it's just the focal point of your mind is turning its attention elsewhere. A person in this stage can both be aware of their inner and outer environment and, even though they are drawn by distractions, if the person has the capability to do so, it is still possible to sustain this energy.

Access Concentration

Access concentration (*Upacara Samadhi*) or neighborhood concentration is a powerful and more enhanced level than momentary concentration. At this second level, the person's mind is fixed on only one object, and does not falter by distractions. A person at this level has great control on their mind, so even if a weak element which may compromise the level of concentration arises, the possibility that the practitioner may gain access to the 3rd level of deeper concentration is still attainable. While at this level, you must be cautious about control of your concentration as it is easy to doze off if not properly handled or unaware.

Absorption Concentration

Absorption concentration (*Appana Samadhi*) is the highest form and most intensive of The Threefold Concentration. People at this level have mastered the first and second levels of concentration and become too engrossed with a subject to ever be distracted. A person who has achieved this level appears more than asleep because their focus is not present in the outer world.

Now we will look at meditation.

Meditation

Meditation is a technique used to develop your consciousness and to train your mind to indulge in clear thoughts without becoming sidetracked or distracted. Unlike concentration, the main purposes of meditation are to find tranquility and inner peace while clearing out all negativity and worries from inside your head. Whether you are experiencing negative or positive thoughts— hindrances— all you need do is calm your senses and obtain peace to achieve meditative absorption. However, for beginners, obtaining peace, or ignoring hindrances, is one of the hardest tasks.

When we meditate, we can gauge our 'level of meditation' (the level we, as an individual are at) in a number of ways; one way is by comparing it against the 4 levels of meditative absorption: in Sanskrit, this is called Jhana (*Dhyana*), and it is a sequence of refined states of mind which leads to impeccable composure and cognizance. We will come onto what this actually is shortly, but the way we gauge this is looking at what hindrances still affect us.

The Five Hindrances

As your proficiency with meditation increases, you will eliminate the following five hindrances to progress through the absorption levels: sensory desire, ill will, sloth and torpor, restlessness and worry, doubt.

We will look at each of these in greater detail in the next chapter, but for now it's good to know that they exist. We will now look at defining the meditative absorption factors.

The Five Meditative Absorption Factors

As mentioned just now, there are 4 meditative absorption levels, the sequence of refined states of mind which leads to impeccable composure and cognizance.

These are inextricably linked to the five factors of meditative absorption. These are: 1) applied thinking, 2) sustained thinking, 3) rapture, 4) bliss, and 5) one-pointedness. In the same way that you must eliminate the five hindrances to progress through the meditative absorption levels, you must also master these factors before you can advance to the next level of absorption— hindrances, meditative absorption factors, and meditative absorption levels are all interlinked.

1. Applied thinking

    The very first factor is applied thinking (*Vitakka*). This is the process of steadying your consciousness onto the theme of meditation, and what you are trying to achieve. Doing so will assist the mind in firmly holding its focus on the desired object.

2. Sustained thinking

    The second factor is sustained thinking (*Vicara*), and its primary function is to sustain and maintain the level of energy achieved during level 1. Your consciousness is already in its meditative state, and sustained thinking will take control allowing you to progress and move to the next level.

3. Rapture

The next factor is called rapture (*Piti*), and is defined as a feeling of complete contentment and peace as a result of performing the meditation correctly—it is momentary joy. Naturally, these feelings are subjective and are governed by the meditator's mind. They come in four forms:

a. Minor rapture

This is a form of short-duration rapture and is experienced by many meditators. It includes the standing-up of hair strands, the out-pouring of tears, and other minor signs.

b. Momentary joy

This form takes on a sudden rush of feelings in the meditator's body. These can often be a tingling sensation or a strange current running through your veins. Again, these are just momentary joys and of short duration.

c. Flood of joy

This third form of rapture is again more powerful, but this one does not remain bound by the meditator's feelings. Those who have experienced it have said that it's actually more like rocking your body as if the ground is moving repeatedly.

d. Transporting rapture

This highest level of rapture makes the practitioner light-headed and causes unintentional body movements. Sometimes, the meditator has even levitated off the ground.

4.   Bliss

If rapture relates to achieving complete contentment in meditation, bliss (*Sukkha*) is directly concerned with gratification in what the meditator has achieved. However, happiness from a blissful state bears no relation to happiness from worldly or material items. Unlike the momentary joys, a blissful state can last for a very long time.

5.   One-pointedness

One-pointedness (*Ekaggata*) is meditative absorption's greatest factor and is achieved only when meditation is performed perfectly. When this occurs, the meditator will experience a sudden feeling of falling deeply somewhere; this is one-pointedness—the ultimate purpose of meditation. However, some have explained that the meditator must refrain from both being anxious or excited here, because either emotion will disengage the meditator from the level of consciousness required to attain one pointedness. Many meditators fail to experience this level because of the sudden rush of emotions.

The Four Absorptions of Meditation

As mentioned above, while practicing meditation, you will experience and take your mind through these different factors towards peace. The factors above relate to the meditative different absorption levels (*the four Jhanas*), and are used in conjunction with the following four levels of absorption to gauge your state of progress:

1. The First Absorption

    The first absorption (*Patthama Jhana*) is the level of meditation where all five factors of meditative absorption are present.

2. The Second Absorption

    To attain the second absorption (*Dutiya Jhana*) applied thinking and sustained thinking have been mastered, but rapture, bliss, and one-pointedness remain.

3. The Third Absorption

    The third absorption (*Tatiya Jhana*) is attained when rapture is also mastered; the remaining factors of absorption are bliss, and one-pointedness.

4. The Fourth Absorption

    When bliss is subdued and mastered, the fourth absorption (*Catuttha Jhana*) is realized, and only equanimity[1] and one-pointedness remain.

---

[1] Equanimity (*Upekkha*) refers to the evenness and unshakeable freedom of mind. It's is self-control, a balanced state-of-mind, strengthened by an absence of strong attachments. In this state, the meditator still notices and cares about events around them, even though they have accepted what is occurring and detached themselves from emotions and feelings.

"Meditation brings wisdom; lack of mediation leaves ignorance. Know well what leads you forward and what holds you back, and choose the path that leads to wisdom."

Lord Buddha

Chapter 3. How to Overcome Obstacles in Meditation

There are many distractions before and during meditation. When you appreciate that meditation is a process where we aim to free our thoughts of all mental and physical negative factors, it stands to reason that if we are unable to clear our thoughts and overcome these obstacles, it will be impossible to achieve our goals and desires. Hence, engaging in meditation means that not only do you need to make a serious and concerted effort towards your success, but you also need to understand what obstacles and hindrances you will be faced with, and how best to overcome them. We touched briefly on these hindrances earlier (page 18), but will now cover them in more detail.

Sensory Desire

Sensory desire (*Kamacchanda*) is the craving for sensual fulfillment. It is the desire to please the five senses: sight, smell, taste, hearing, and physical touch, all of which lead to distraction in meditation. For instance, imagine you are in the middle of your practice and you suddenly hear a whistling sound. Your sense of hearing stimulates your brain to open your eyes and locate where the sound is coming from. Eventually, your whole attention is focused on this noise and your thoughts and focus are gone from where they should be—they are lost. This particular hindrance also relates to other forms of desire, such as lust and other means of sexual gratification through touch, sight, or smell. Indeed, gluttony is another factor as your hunger for food incorporates desires to satiate your sense of taste.

To overcome sensory desire, you should acknowledge the presence of the particular desire in question, and then focus on that subject alone. If you acknowledge and convince yourself that this desire does actually exist, instead of giving in and being distracted, you can apply techniques to overcome it.

Some techniques to achieve this include acknowledging and noticing the distraction, and then letting it go. For example, you can take notice of a noise or other distraction and then repeat the distraction in your mind, "The dog is barking, the dog is barking..." and the distraction will eventually disappear. This applies to any sensory desire. Whatever feeling occurs, appears, or touches you, notice it, repeat it in your mind, and it will remove itself.

It is important to remember that our mind is more powerful than all of these desires, and separating ourselves from worldly gratification is a step on the path to experiencing the meditative absorptions (*Jhana*).

Ill Will

Ill will (*Vyapada*) is the desire to dwell on negative strong feelings against other people. As it's not related to the physical senses, but rather to one's emotions or feelings, it is the opposite of sensory desire. Some of these feelings include bitterness, anger, rejection, and a desire to avenge and hurt the person who has harmed you; but, also it's where you hold resentment, regret, and guilt about yourself: ill will is about holding onto unforgiving thoughts.

According to Ajarn Brahmayamso, the remedy to this kind of hindrance is to meditate on the positive feeling of loving kindness (*Metta*). Consequently, instead of fighting with these emotions, rather focus on the feelings themselves and then replace them with compassion and deep sympathy towards daily battles the other person faces. Looking to understand why that particular person hurt you, instead of magnifying their flaws and wrong-doings, is one effective way of redeeming yourself from ill will. Furthermore, it will also lead you towards forgiveness and provide a great opportunity to build a meaningful and loving relationship with others, towards nature, and maybe even to reflect some of it back onto yourself.

Sloth and Torpor

Sloth and torpor (*Thina* and *Middha*), refers to the heaviness of the body and the dullness of the mind, both of which may result in drowsiness during the meditation process. If you are not aware of the initial signs of this hindrance, it will most likely lead you to falling asleep. It is this type of impediment that saps your enthusiasm towards meditation, and drains your energy from concentration, leading you to becoming tired, bored, or both.

To prevent this, before meditating, it is important to have a keen interest in the process as well as a firm goal. This way, you will motivate yourself to achieve your focus and attention. If you do recognize a certain heaviness in your body, or dullness of the mind, then stop for a moment, go for a short walk, or even wash your face to refresh yourself before returning to your meditation. Persisting with the practice while stressing over it is counterproductive.

Restlessness and Worry

Restlessness and worry (*Uddhacca* and *Kukkucca*), refer to the state of mind where the meditator cannot find contentment with anything. It is an anxious attitude driven by a desire to achieve more rather than being satisfied with what you currently have. A prime example is being agitated and then rushing to jump to the next stage of meditation instead of appreciating your presence and achievements in the current process. When this occurs, you're more concerned about how to get to the next level of meditative absorption than you are of doing this level correctly.

Most of us have experienced these obstacles, and the answer is quite simple. These kinds of thoughts lead to total distraction and the best way to overcome such force is to develop an attitude of contentment towards the simple things: be grateful with what you have, instead of magnifying and being concerned with what you don't.

Doubt

Doubt (*Vicikiccha*) refers to the series of unsettling inner questions which occur at a time when you should be moving deeper into silent meditation. Doubt is where you question the ability of a person, the effectiveness of a process, or even interrogate yourself if you have difficulty in producing something positive. Doubt is embracing a building fear inside your heart and mind, rather than embracing the challenge to attain your goal.

You should take clear instruction to overcome doubt in meditation, and learn the necessary procedures correctly. That way, you will develop your confidence in what you do and what you can achieve without any second thoughts. To this end, having a good, trustworthy meditation coach or teacher is a huge aid for a new meditator. The teacher can then nurture you and help build your confidence.

Chapter 4. Concentration and Meditation Practices

The practice of meditation is extremely important in reducing stress levels and improving focus, as well as developing a strong spiritual connection, regardless of your religious beliefs. This practice has been an essential part of Buddhism and Hinduism, for many years (including yogic practices). There are several different elements and aspects to meditation, including breathing, concentration, and meditation itself; and, you can easily incorporate these traditions into your life to feel both stronger and happier.

Mindfulness of Breathing

Mindfulness of breathing (*Anapanasati*), is a more in-depth focus on the actual breath in meditation—it can also be called breath-based practice. It is an extremely important element in most forms of Buddhism, and has been incorporated into many meditation techniques.

There are many ways to practice mindfulness of breathing, and one of the most common methods is to focus on the breath in cycles of ten-counts. So, the meditator would inhale for a count of ten, then exhale for a count of ten. This creates a rhythm that allows the meditator to focus on their bodily sensations as well as their mental processes. After focusing on the counting, the meditator will then focus on the presence of the breath within the body. They will be aware of the breath as it travels through the nose and the mouth, in through the lungs, and out through the extremities. From there, one can drill-down and focus on the presence of breath as it goes through specific parts of the body. Doing so can improve focus, and can also be used to relax specific muscles or relieve pain. This has been a very important part of Yogic practice.

Traditionally, the practitioner is aware of their natural breath without either forcing or changing it. As part of the practice, they will notice if their breath is short or long, and will make note of it without passing any judgement or changing it. This can be practiced in a sitting position or while standing, and it is recommended that someone new to mindfulness of breathing begins with ten or fifteen minute practice sessions and then work their way up from there.

There are sixteen stages of mindfulness of breathing, and they are divided into four groups (tetrads of stages). Traditionally, and regardless of the level of experience, all meditation sessions should begin with the first stage and work their way through the tetrads.

1. The first tetrad focuses on the body. The meditator first focuses on short and long breaths to gain awareness of their natural rhythms. Then, they will breathe with an awareness of their entire body in order to separate the breath from the rest of their bodily sensations. Finally, they will focus on tranquillity of the body, in order to reach a state of calmness and relaxation.

2. The second tetrad focuses on feelings. The first stage in this tetrad, is the experience of rapture: connecting the meditator with their feelings, particularly those of inspiration and excitement. From there, in this second tetrad, you move into a state of bliss—a deeper sense of joy. The meditator then lets themselves fully experience these mental activities without change or judgement; and, finally, the meditator tranquilizes their mental state, absorbing these feelings of rapture and bliss.

3. In the third tetrad, the meditator focuses on the heart and mind, primarily by focusing on their positive qualities and energy. Then, they center the mind in a mild state of concentration, which allows the meditator to remain fully involved in their practice. To talk through this process thus far, in the first tetrad, the meditator experienced their mental state; in the second tetrad this expands to gladdening the mind; and now, in the third tetrad, the meditator is able to release their mind, and achieves a wonderful state of liberation.

4. Now the mind has been liberated, the fourth tetrad focuses on the four states of contemplation: impermanence, fading of lust, cessation of involvement, and relinquishment of involvement. At this stage, the meditator will experience the full benefits of mindfulness of breathing, including peace, insight, freedom, calmness, and centeredness.

Right Concentration

One important form of meditation is right concentration (*Samma Samadhi*). In Buddhism, this is the eighth and final step of the Eightfold Path— the spiritual journey to end suffering. Buddhist monks use right concentration to strengthen their character and other aspects of their lives.

If you remember back to Chapter 2, where we talked about concentration and meditation, those wishing to achieve a state of right concentration must, first, find a space clear of distractions, and then they must find an object on which to concentrate. The basis of this meditation comes from an intense focus on this object. Buddhist meditation manuals suggest different objects which may work more successfully for different personality types.

After the meditator has selected their object, they must then choose a tranquil, distraction-free spot in which to concentrate. The traditional Buddhist meditation position is sitting with legs crossed, with their hands folded in their lap, with good posture through the back, and their eyes closed. Breathing should remain even and full and, by picturing your chosen object and saying the name of that object in your mind, focus should remain fixed. If your mind strays, you should be sure to refocus as quickly as possible, until eventually your mind no longer wanders and your focus is secure. On this path to concentration, as you are likely to encounter many distractions and challenges within your mind, patience is very important.

Once your focus is clear and steady, your mind is free of any distractions, and you have mastered momentary concentration and access concentration—the first two levels of The Threefold Concentration—the meditator can then start to go through absorption concentration—the third And last level of threefold concentration (which is also equivalent to the 1st level of absorption meditation). At this point, the concept of the object will start to become very strong and clear in your mind.

1. The first step, the first absorption (refer to *The Four Absorptions of Meditation*, on page 20), is a state of composure and focus.

2. From there, the mind transitions into the second absorption, which is a state of withdrawal from the physical world, and this creates the states of rapture and pleasure.

3. The third absorption is a state of pleasant, tranquil mindfulness.

4. The fourth absorption is a sort of purity of the mind, where no positive or negative emotions or senses are felt.

As first discussed in section 2.2.2, there are five positive mental factors in Buddhism that will help the meditator through these first four stages: initial focus on the object (applied thinking), retention of focus on the object (sustained thinking), joy and rapture (rapture), happiness (bliss), and unifying the mind (one-pointedness). With these positive mental factors, the daunting task of achieving right concentration is made much easier.

Buddhist monks use these practices for a number of positive reasons: it is said to create wisdom and insight, and to liberate the mind from the troubles of the physical world. The final step on the Eightfold Path to Enlightenment it is a final sense of freedom from suffering, and a transcendence of the distractions of the world.

Again, the concentration practice focuses on oneness with a chosen object which can either be a deliberative or a reflective object. A deliberative object is something physical and perceptible, such as an image of a deity, water or earth, etc. Whereas a reflective object is imperceptible and is more of a concept, such as a chakra, or one's own breathe. After the object has been chosen and focused upon, the meditator can then work towards achieving their goal.

The main task of concentration is to learn to focus the mind on one object without letting distractions creep in. This is extremely challenging and requires significant effort to practice. But, because it can be difficult, the rewards of successful concentration are extremely high; and, one who successfully masters this practice will experience a sense of calm, wisdom, and awareness of both mind and body.

Tranquillity Meditation

Similar to right concentration, the practice of tranquility meditation (*Samatha Panna*), is a Buddhist practice that focuses on soothing the mind and body through concentration on breath. The word *Samatha* means "calm", and *Panna* means "developing wisdom"; and, their main goal is to achieve a sense of calmness through focus on breath in order to develop wisdom. Because the focus on the natural rhythm of one's breath helps simplify thoughts as well as clearing out confusing and distracting stressors, it can help the meditator to feel a sense of clarity in their life. Indeed, true focus on the breath creates a sense of peace, happiness, and one-ness with your own body.

The Nine Stages of Mental Abiding

In the practice of tranquility meditation, there are nine stages of training the mind—or "mental abiding"—through which the meditator will be able to access a calm and tranquil mind.

1. The first stage is the placement of the mind. Here, though the meditator focuses on their object of concentration (this is traditionally on the cycle of breath through the

torso) they often struggle to maintain that focus. Until they can maintain it, they will remain in the first stage.

2. When the beginner can focus on their breath for about a minute, the second stage of continuous attention has been attained. At this point, the meditator is seeing a drastic improvement and is therefore feeling more motivated with the practice and towards reaching an eventual state of total calm.

3. When the meditator can maintain their focus for almost the entire duration of their practice session, they have reached the third stage of repeated attention. Here they are still aware of distractions, but their increased awareness means they are able to correct it immediately when it happens. The meditator will start to enjoy a real feeling of relaxation, although they are still very far from achieving true calm.

4. The fourth stage of calm attention occurs when the meditator can completely maintain their focus for an hour-long practice session without any distractions. At this point, there are still subtle occurrences of dullness of the mind or excitation.

5. The next stage, tamed attention, occurs when a deep sense of relaxation begins. Often during this stage, the meditator will mistakenly define mental laxity for calm. This must be avoided as much as possible.

6. The stage of pacified attention occurs only after the meditator has trained consistently for hundreds of hours and has mastered control over occurrences of mental fogginess or laxity. At this point, the awareness of senses and emotions is deeply diminished.

7. Fully pacified attention occurs when instances of mental excitation or dullness are extremely rare. The meditator has a very sharp awareness of these elements and can correct them immediately. At this point, the meditator can focus for several hours at a time.

8. The eighth stage is single-pointed attention, and occurs when this strong meditative state can be reached with ease.

9. The final stage to tranquillity meditation is attentional balance, and occurs when the meditator can focus for hours at a time with complete ease and no distractions.

After reaching the 9th, final, stage of calmness, the meditator can start to proceed with the 1st of the 4 levels of meditative absorption (*the 4 jhanas*).

From this state of calmness, the meditator will feel a sense of great lightness and openness. It is from here that they can proceed onto the intense focus of concentration. The focus on breath and calm through the body that has been achieved here is also extremely beneficial to one's physical health, because it rids the body of unnecessary tension that can cause health problems.

Insight Meditation

While tranquility meditation focuses on calmness, the meditation practice of insight meditation or Vipassana Panna focuses on developing a sense of thoughtfulness about the world. This style of meditation has become very popular in the Western world and is known as "mindfulness meditation". The word Vipassana means "to see things as they really are", and Panna means "developing wisdom". Thus, these forms of meditation focus on clarity of the mind during which the Three Characteristics are discovered and contemplated: impermanence, suffering, and non-self-awareness (emptiness). They are considered the three most important insights into the true nature of reality. This is a very introspective meditation practice and, as such, has become a popular way of processing difficult emotional situations.

As mentioned in Chapter 2.2.3, there are four meditative absorptions in insight meditation: the first stage/first absorption, is an exploration of mind and body where the meditator focuses on how they affect each other. In the second absorption, the trials of the first stage slowly dissipate, and the practice begins to feel effortless; feelings of rapture, joy, and bliss are common in this stage. In the third absorption, these feelings leave, and a sense of true happiness and tranquillity is left. Finally, the fourth absorption is characterized by a unity of the mind and openness to knowledge and wisdom.

Like tranquillity meditation, insight meditation also focuses on the mindfulness of breathing. However, instead of focusing on it in a way that creates complete calm, insight meditation focuses on the breath as a catalyst for introspection. The main goal is to gain insight into the true nature of reality. Impermanence is a very important concept here because it emphasizes how changeable and fragile life is. The meditator is encouraged to notice these things and, due to the ever-changing nature of the universe and because our pain and suffering is insubstantial and will change, to then let them go.

Insight meditation is traditionally done in a place of calm, such as a forest or under a tree (if you can get that close to nature); but any quiet place should suffice. The posture here is the same as in right concentration and tranquillity meditation, sitting with legs crossed and an upright back. Here your focus is on the rise and fall of your breath. However, unlike these previous methods, for insight meditation, interruptions or distractions should be noted, and again let go. Choosing simple words to note experiences and mental objects is best, as they can be incorporated into the rhythm of the breath. After a session of insight meditation, this practice can be carried over into one's daily activities.

Daily Meditation Practices

Now we've come this far, the question is how do we incorporate these complicated practices into our everyday life? Well, the easiest way is to set aside a manageable amount of time every day to dedicate to meditation practice, 10 minutes will do to start. It is best to meditate at the same time every day because that will help turn this new practice into a habit. Furthermore, it is also a good idea to set aside a specific quiet space for your meditation; and, when you start, make sure you are suitably clothed and in a comfortable position that you will be able to maintain—remember, the main goal in the beginning is to focus your mind.

If you haven't skipped chapters to come to this page, you now realize that lack of focus is the most common problem for beginners, so it helps to pick a really strong image to focus on at first. Focusing on your breath works really well for many people, and is a principle reason why breath-based practice or mindfulness of breathing is so popular all over the world. If you prefer, you can also stare at an image or an object: many find that lighting a candle is both an aid to focus, as well helping to create a mood conducive to meditation.

When you start, try to remove your mind from yourself. Observe your body's sensations and feelings, but don't let yourself be present in these feelings. Imagine you are a person outside of your body looking down from above, and calmly watching yourself. This does take a bit of practice, and it will probably help you to find guided meditation to follow; but, there are many recordings on the Internet that are perfect for just this. They can be found through YouTube, podcasts on iTunes, or just a simple Google search.

Once you have mastered mindfulness of breathing, you can try focusing your breath through different parts of your body. Some people start at the head and work down to the feet, or vice versa. If you do have trouble calming your mind this may actually help you, as instead of trying to empty your mind completely on the first try, it gives you something to focus on while you are meditating.

I hope you realize that these are just basic steps towards an eventual bigger meditation goal of right concentration, tranquility meditation, and insight meditation; and all these practices can be performed through mindfulness of breathing. What is important is you take your time, and you work through the steps as slowly and as thoroughly as you need to, to enable you to have a quality and meaningful meditation experience. These states of concentration, calm, and insight will never be mastered overnight (and many spend their entire lives working towards mastery); but you can and will see very fast initial results. Within a very short time of working through the steps, you will most likely see an improvement in both your mental state and your physical health, which will help enormously in motivating you to continue towards your goal.

Finally, the wide variety of meditation styles make them applicable to people from all walks of life; so, no matter your culture, age, career, or circumstance, you can benefit from meditation. Whether it's just a simple, daily 5 minute breathing exercise, or a dedicated study of right concentration, you will develop your sense of self, your understanding of the world, and your health.

Conclusion

In conclusion, I hope you've enjoyed reading my books. I also hope that now you've looked at the principle aspects of both Buddhism and meditation, I am confident that by understanding and implementing the topics we've covered, you will see how either one may perhaps assist you in looking at, evaluating, and improving your own particular situation and (if you do indeed need to do so).

Regardless of whether you are actually a Buddhist yourself, or whether or not you practice meditation regularly, I hope you can see that by making small changes to your daily routine, and perhaps by adopting some of these practices, they will not only help to improve your life, but can help in other areas, such as: your outlook, your relationships with others, with how you view your surroundings, with those whom you come into contact with, and of course your health.

Author's Page

Duangta Wanthong Mondi is Thai and a Buddhist. She lives and works in the North-east of Thailand as an English teacher in a Thai State school.

Duangta has an M. Ed. In Teaching English as a Foreign Language (TEFL), and has co-authored a series of books to help English speakers learn Thai.

The series is called *Quest (**Quick, Easy, Simple Thai**)* and consists of:

- Learning Thai, Your Great Adventure

- Learn Thai Alphabet with Memory Aids to Your Great Adventure

- The Perfect Thai Phrasebook

- How to Read Thai

- The Learn Thai Alphabet application (web/iPad app)

- The Learn Thai Numbers application (web/iPad app)

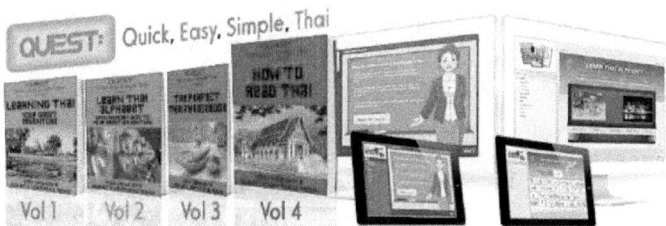

Website – *http://www.teachermondi.com*

Facebook - *https://www.facebook.com/teachermondi*

Check out my author page on Amazon

(amazon.com/author/duangtamondi)

Please Leave a Review on Amazon

Finally, if you have enjoyed the book, I would be most grateful if you would leave a review on Amazon: without reviews, authors like me really struggle. So you would not only be helping others, but me too.